Experience of Select Regulatory Bodies in Higher Education in India

Experience of Select Regulatory Bodies in Higher Education in India

Mohammad Sohail

ADROIT

Adroit Publishers

NEW DELHI • KATHMANDU

ISBN : 978-81-87393-65-8

2019

Published by
ADROIT PUBLISHERS 4675/21, Ganpati Bhawan, Ansari Road, Daryaganj, New Delhi-110 002 Phone : 011-23266030
adroitpublishers@gmail.com

Typeset in Garamond Premier Pro by Arun, Akriti Graphic Solution, Delhi-110081 E-mail: arun263923@gmail.com, Ph: 9999414390

Preface

Higher education is increasingly emerging as a trusted engine of socio-economic development. The contribution of higher education in the socio-economic development of a country is better understood in the light of positive externalities produced by it. The positive externalities of higher education can be discussed under three major categories i.e. economic, social and health benefits for others. The economic benefits include higher tax collections which are used by the governments to provide various services to the citizens; low unemployment rate; quality workforce and increased economic growth. The social benefits consist of better people's participation; increased donations to charities; low crime rates; improved sense of volunteerism; and effective racial tolerance. The health benefits are in the form of low cigarette consumption rate and increase in blood donations (Toutkoushian and Paulsen, 2016). The blending of human capital theory and emergence of knowledge economy has made the contribution of higher education in the socio-economic development of a country more pronounced. In order to steer higher education in the right direction for making it a reliable source of socio-economic development, quality of higher education is of paramount importance. The quality concerns in higher education are also looked after by the system of regulation. Further, regulation plays a pivotal role in determining, maintaining and coordinating quality standards in higher education. Regulation of higher education is also desired for introducing, implementing and monitoring public policies aimed at nurturing higher education to continue playing its role in the socio-economic development.

A country like India which is the third largest higher education system in terms of student enrolment and number of higher education institutes and has rich demographic dividend, well directed regulation of higher education is a need of the hour for achieving higher rate of socio-economic development. Effective regulatory mechanism in higher education in India is also necessary to successfully address the various challenges Indian higher education system is facing.

Higher education in India is being regulated by around 18 regulatory bodies. Major bodies include the University Grants Commission (UGC), All India Council of Technical Education (AICTE), Medical Council of India (MCI), Indian Council for Agricultural Research (ICAR), National Council for Teacher Education (NCTE), Dental Council of India (DCI), Pharmacy Council of India (PCI), Indian Nursing Council (INC) and Bar Council of India (BCI). Except the University Grants Commission, each regulatory body has the responsibility of regulating specific field of study.

The regulatory mechanism in higher education in India is facing severe criticism from various stakeholders. Two of the important reports relating to higher education in India, namely, Yash Pal Committee Report (2009) and National Knowledge Commission Report (2009) have found that the Indian higher education is over regulated and yet less governed. The issues of inefficacy, overlapping and contradiction are also looming large. The mediocre quality of higher education exhibited in the form of low ranking of Indian institutes in the world university ranking survey is also partly attributed to the ineffective regulatory mechanism.

The voices of reforming the existing regulatory mechanism are becoming louder and louder. Various Committees have proposed the abolition of the multiple regulatory bodies and instead set up one umbrella regulator. The National Knowledge Commission Report named the regulatory authority as Independent Regulatory Authority for Higher Education and Yash Pal Committee Report termed the same as National Commission for Higher Education and Research. The present government had also set up Committees to revamp the regulatory mechanism in higher education. The Committees have signalled towards setting up an umbrella regulator. However in the recent move, the Government has proposed to replace the individual regulatory bodies with new agencies. For example, the UGC has been proposed to be replaced by the Higher Education Commission of India. As per the reports, similar process will be initiated in case of AICTE. It is in this backdrop that the present study has utmost contemporary relevance. The study was conducted in the year 2012 as Masters Dissertation. The study takes into account the experience of three major regulatory bodies namely, the UGC, the AICTE and the MCI. The study besides evaluating the role of these regulatory bodies in fulfilling their respective mandates, also enlist the challenges faced by these bodies. Policy prescriptions for improving the regulatory role of these bodies are also part of this study.

Contents

Preface v

1. Introduction 1
2. University Grants Commission (U.G.C) as a Regulator: 26
   Introduction, Structure, Functioning and Evaluation
   of the Role
3. All India Council for Technical Education (AICTE): 61
   Emergence, Structure, functioning and its Evaluation
4. Medical Council of India: As a Regulator; 89
   Introduction, organization, functioning and
   its assessment
5. Summary, Conclusions and Policy Prescriptions 110

Index 127

1

Introduction

Education in general and higher education in specific has been an effective instrument for overall development. In India higher education is provided both by the public and private sector. After economic liberalization the role of private sector in higher education has increased tremendously. The growing presence of private sector in the provision of higher education provides a justifiable rationale for regulating higher education sector effectively. Already regulatory policies and organization are in place. However their multiplicity and overlapping role has made the higher education system over-governed and ineffective in the delivery of good quality higher education across all strata of society. It is in this backdrop that the present study is conceived. This chapter includes the role of higher education in development, the concept of regulation and rationale for the regulation in the field of higher education. The chapter also deals with review of literature, significance of the study, objectives of the study, research methodology and chapterization.

Role of Higher Education in Development

Education from the earlier times has been considered as a main source, facilitating development particularly economic development, and that in case of higher education is considered to be the main factor in achieving the economic development.[1]

Over the period of time the world believed that the country which has more man power will lead the world, and this view was quiet genuine. Following the essence of this approach layman thought of, having more population leads to the development, as it adds more to the man power. However the approach had some improvements and later it was said and observed that the country having quality man power has a greater chance to develop. The difference between having a greater man power and quality man power is very important. So the human resource development is the main area of concern. Education facilitates the human resource development by placing institutional and functional arrangement in the society. There is no doubt that what led to the sincerity of human resource in relation to development was the outcome of human capital theory. Human capital theory postulates the dialectical relationship between higher education and development policies and it is the same theory which enunciates that education is the main instrument in the economic development of countries. The contribution of higher education in the economic development occurs when the human capital acts as the most important element of production. One of the roles that education is urged to play is to study the reasons of deficiency in achieving the aims of economic development, reconsider the educational system to improve the quality and efficiency of education to comply to the development needs, taking into consideration that education is a process of investing the human capital that revenues individuals and society as any investment project.[2]

1. Hisham Al-Smadi, Abdel Salam Njadat (2009), "The Role of Higher Education in the Economic Development of the Hashemite Kingdom of Jordan", *Middle Eastern Finance and Economics*, Issue 3, Euro Journals Publishing, Inc.
2. ibid

The other interesting factor is the dynamic nature of technology and ongoing development and research in this area, and it is only through the medium of education in general and especially the higher education that the countries made themselves up to date in the technological aspect and also made its man power up to date to these new innovations. Thus education also plays essential role in managing development, enhancing production, and developing innovation. Education does not only comply with the social desire or an intellectual luxury, and it does not anymore present only a country service, but education became a wide domain for investment, complies with the needs of development, progress and promotion. Education is always considered as a productive investment.[3]

The objective of having knowledge economy is also consequence of the good quality of higher education institution in the country. Which growth path India embarks on in the future will depend on how well the government, private sector, and civil society can work together to create a common understanding of where the economy should be headed and what it needs to get there. India can no doubt reap tremendous economic gains by developing policies and strategies that focus on making more effective use of knowledge to increase the overall productivity of the economy and the welfare of its population. In so doing, India will be able to improve its international competitiveness and join the ranks of countries that are making a successful transition to the knowledge economy.[4]

In Indian context the role of higher education in development is more critical. There can be no doubt that higher education has made a significant contribution to economic development, social progress and political democracy in independent India. It is a source of dynamism

3. ibid
4. Carl Dahlman and Anuja Utz (2004),"India and the Knowledge Economy: Leveraging Strengths and Opportunities", Finance and Private Sector Development Unit of the World Bank's South Asia Region and The World Bank Institute.

for the economy. Higher education has provided social opportunities to people. Higher education is also taken as an instrument fostering democracy in our polity. It has initiated the transition of the society in order to create a knowledge society.[5]

The situation of the Indian economy from the world perspective is that India is one of the fast growing economies in the world and India has the human capital of 550 million below the age of 25. However, India's ability to positively react to these aspects largely depends on the education system it has. As we have observed above that however it is assumed plus point to have more man power but it is useless if this man power is not equipped with quality education that automatically leads to technological advancement, skill development of the society. India is a developing country where societal transformation and economic transformation under modernization are taking place so it is highly important to address the issue of quality education.

On the role of higher education we can conclude that a competitive economy can only be based on a well-educated population as well as dynamic research and development (R&D) sector. The two components of knowledge; the human capital and the technology have become central to economic development. In the age of globalization, the knowledge economy discourse has become a way to characterize the new relationship between the state, society and economy and rendered higher education increasingly important for the international competitiveness of nation states through their central task of generation, application and dissemination of knowledge and training high skilled labour force.[6]

---

5. Government of India (2009), "National Knowledge Commission: Report to the Nation", National Knowledge Commission, New Delhi
6. Irena Macerinskiene, Birute Vaiksnoraite (2006), "The Role OF Higher Education to Economic Development", VADYBA / MANAGEMENT. 2006 m. Nr. 2(11), www.leidykla.eu/fileadmin/Vadyba/11/Irena_Macerinskiene_Birute_Vaiksnoraite.pdf

Regulation

Education is provided by both public and private. In India access to higher education is around 25 percent. It is aimed to double it by the end of the 12th Five Year Plan (2012-17).

The government sector due to financial distress cannot provide sufficient funds for achieving the set target. Therefore the government has invited the private capital. The growing role of private sector in higher education necessitates having effective regulation of education sector. Prior to explaining the rationale of regulation of education sector it is desirable to discuss the concept of regulation.

Regulatory mechanism works as a medium of positive governmental intervention in the service of various socio-economic goods. The belief that the government which governs the least is the best, regulation is the way that provides any government by which it can positively intervene in the state economy. Regulation can be seen as an outcome of the State v/s Market debate, which preferred and suggested the government to play the role of a regulator. This also came as an alternative to the over burdening of government's activities. With the introduction of liberalization and privatization, regulation became more prominent.

Regulation as mandated by the government or state attempts to produce outcomes which otherwise might not occur, produce or prevents outcomes in different places to what might otherwise occur, or produce or prevent outcomes in different timescales than would otherwise occur. Regulations rarely produces complete outcomes or prevent outcomes completely but they generally do modify what would otherwise take place. Common examples of regulation include attempts to control market entries, prices, wages, pollution effects, employment for certain people in certain industries, standards of production for certain goods and services.[7]

7. http://en.wikipedia.org/wiki/regulation of Wikipedia-The Free Encyclopedia

Defining it in another way "Regulation is also defined as the rules enforced by a government agency to restrict or control economic activity in price-setting, product standards, trading standards and the conditions under which firms can enter an industry."[8]

Regulation in Higher Education: Rationale

Regulation as stated above seems as a controlling factor that concentrates on price-setting, better service delivery, and better trading standards and makes regulation for the entry of new firms in the area of socio-economic goods. Now taking the institution of higher education, the need of regulatory mechanism grows further in this arena. Higher education is no longer perceived as an acquisition of a degree but an instrument to obtain sufficient knowledge and skills so as to function as a productive member of the society. The structure and delivery of higher education is changing, including the coming up of new types of educational institutions and an increasing use of technology that allows institutions to operate on a national and global scale. Also, Higher education has explicitly acquired an economic value in today's knowledge economy. All these changes have resulted in growing demand for increased accountability.[9]

Taking into consideration the rationale behind the regulation of higher education, we study the reasons through the following aspects;

1. Service delivery
2. Privatization
3. Globalization

---

8. Akshat Mehta (2009), *Regulatory Governance In The Deregulated Telecom Sector: An Assessment of the Role of Telecom Regulatory Authority of India (PH.D Thesis),* Department of Public Administration, Panjab University, Chandigarh (India), p.57.
9. Pawan Aggarwal (2006), "higher Education in India; Need for Change", Working Paper no. 180, Indian Council for Research on International Economic Relations, *New Delhi*

Service Delivery

Though the changing structure and delivery of higher education and increasing use of technology are creating a competitive market for higher education, the total reliance on market forces alone in higher education is not the most feasible option. While the market forces are being increasingly used the world over to coordinate and steer the higher education system, yet the limitations are also becoming clearer. Rising inequities, increasing exploitation of gullible students, deteriorating standards and skewed growth necessitate government intervention. The limitations of market forces in higher education need to be understood and a regulatory system must be developed to overcome these limitations.[10]

Universities have been working as a main service delivering institutions in the area of higher education. But this system has suffered from many drawbacks. Universities remain one of the most under-managed organizations in our society. The governance structures are archaic and have not changed with changing environment to meet the expectation of its various stakeholders. While most other organization in the society have adapted themselves in terms of organizational designs, mechanisms for conducting their business and motivating people, use of technology to bring effectiveness in operations etc., but universities have not changed much in this aspect.[11]

The National Knowledge Commission's main area of focus and the five key aspects of knowledge: enhancing access to knowledge, reinvigorating institutions where knowledge concepts are imparted, creating a world class environment for creation of knowledge, promoting applications of knowledge for sustained and inclusive

---

10. *Ibid*
11. Government of India (2008 a), *"Report of 'The Committee to Advise on Renovation and Rejuvenation of Higher Education", department of Higher Education, Ministry of Human Resource Development, New Delhi.*

growth and using knowledge application in efficient delivery of public services, are also the concerns that highlight the need of regulation in the field of higher education and its service delivery aspect.

The service delivery system in higher education and need for regulation in this regard is further highlighted by two aspects, namely, the accountability and autonomy of higher education institutes. Interference, from various political or commercial vested interests, in the functioning of the universities comes in many different forms and intensities. It touches all aspects of higher education and involves improper admission of students, pressure in selection of teachers, manipulation in appointment of seniors functionaries like vice-chancellors, Registrars and deans, purchase of equipment and allotment of construction contracts and so on.[12]

The Kothari Commission recognized the imperatives of higher education autonomy and cautioned that, "only an autonomous institution, free from regimentation of ideas and pressure of party or power politics, can pursue truth fearlessly and build up in its teachers and students, habits of independent thinking and spirit of enquiry unfettered by the limitations and prejudices of the near and immediate which is also essential for the development of a free society. The knowledge commission report has also presented its concern over the matter of autonomy and accountability of higher education institutes". Quality assurance and fee mechanism are other factors that also favor regulation in the service delivery aspect. The accreditation and affiliation system in higher education and the sudden spurt in the newly established educational institutes as the deemed university are also the concerns that needs a regulatory mechanism.[13]

The system of Regulation oversees the whole service delivery process and every aspect beginning from the admission procedure as

12. *ibid*
13. ibid

well. The regulation in this regard includes; defining the regulation during the admission process, controlling fee structure, funding of the institutions, describing minimum standard for the faculty, teaching and examination, monitoring the developments in the field of collegiate and university from time to time, catering to the challenges of expansion and diversification. The expansion of the higher education system, followed by the diversification was the main challenge in front of the regulatory mechanism. The regulatory mechanism thus performs its functioning in all areas of higher education system, be it technical education, humanities, social sciences, physical sciences, life sciences, management, commerce etc. So the service delivery aspect of higher education has been one of the major factor contributing to the realization of the need of regulatory mechanism in higher education system.

Privatization

Privatization and commercialization of higher education builds a suitable case of regulation of higher education, so that the private players should not only overcharge fee but also deliver good quality education to all strata of society. According to Yash Pal Committee report, "in fact we recognize the need for different layers of institutions in the field of higher education, including state-run, private and those established through public-private partnership. What is required in order to make all of them work efficiently and serve overall national goals is the framing of rational and consistent ground rules overseen by a transparent regulatory mechanism. The economic reforms after 1991 and in the wake of privatization and liberalization, the institution of higher education was also under its effect. The government's inability to fulfill the increased demand in the area of higher education, Government's financial constraints and privatization as an alternative to these problems paved the way for the entry of private players in higher education system". The state's failure or unresponsiveness in regard to cater the expansion in the sectors of higher education, the gap was filled by the private players.

However, there has been no policy or guidelines to measure the competence of private investors in starting and managing a technical institution other than the requirement that it should be registered as non-profit or charitable trust or society. This lacuna has been exploited by many investors, who have no understanding or experience of the responsibilities associated with institutions of higher education. The trusts or societies that have been formed largely consists of immediate family members-some of whom had little or no educational background-with some exceptions.[14]

The experience with the privatization of higher education has brought two kinds of viewpoints. Some considers them as the panacea for higher education. They do not want any kind of regulation and interference in the establishment and operation of private institutions and would let the market forces determine their survival. There are many others who consider private institutions as the fountain of malpractices, exploitation and poor quality, which are manipulated politically or financially. Clearly both perceptions are based on real world experiences though these may suffer from undue generalization. It would be unfair to characterize all self-financing private institutions as indulging in undesirable practices.[15]

However some of the private institutions in India like of Tata Institute of Social Sciences, and Tata Institute of Fundamental Research (which later became deemed universities) have set examples for other institutes, the way they have performed so far, the way they have managed their financial matters from admission fee to tuition fee, scholarships, the quality of research, their international recognition, the faculty standard and the standards of students are unmatchable.

14. ibid
15. *Pawan Aggarwal, op. cit.*

There are many institutes of this kind in India. But this is one of the aspects while other aspects also shows the exploitative and corrupt measure adapted by the private institutes through all investments on the institution and all appointments and service conditions and to a considerable extent most decisions on admission of students in management quota have been under control of such family trusts or societies. The cost of receiving higher education from these institutions is affordable to elite strata of the society only. The experience of privatization of higher education in Punjab shows that many of the private institutions in the field of management and engineering which were set up on leased lands, later turned into the marriage palaces, because of the unavailability of students. Then also the case of paid degrees in masters and even in Ph.Ds. came into light, describing the miserable plight of these private institutions and the ignorance on the part of the governments. From this point of view we feel the need of having strict and well defined regulatory mechanism which will define the measures and eligibility criteria for the entry of new private institutions in the field of higher education will have regular check on their performance, control on their profit maximization abilities and which will assure the quality of their services.

Globalization

The modern world has turned itself into a global village. Countries are influenced by the developments taking place in other parts of the world. The effects of globalization has become more visible and convincing on the higher education system over the period of time. There is a debate being carried about the positive and negative aspects of globalization on higher education system. In this backdrop the regulation of globalization of higher education becomes significant and much demanded. No doubt, higher education has attained a key position in the knowledge society under globalized economy. However, the challenges faced are immense and far reaching. Its impact on the clientele and individual, institution, systems and societies is not only ambiguous but also not comprehendible at this moment unless it is viewed in the context of various other factors that are simultaneously operating on higher education system. The ambiguity and non comprehendible nature of the effects of globalization of higher education is due to the pros and cons of this aspect. This also makes the state to decide on either to explore the option of globalization of higher education or not. So it has been one of the main concerns of the state to devise the mechanism which can make the globalization beneficial to their system of education. The aspect of globalization has created two types of view points; some are of the view that the rapid cross national flow of people, goods, capital and information may dissolve the nation state, push institutions of higher education into a common mould where as other disagree with this view. The followers of second view point take globalization as a challenge to the higher education system. The comparison between these two viewpoints further state that it is assumed that globalization promises dramatic and rewarding change to their education system, of societies which are relatively stable in their political, social and institutional makeup, while for others it may threaten the very stability needed to build well performing higher education system. It is also true, that so far globalization has given the advanced economies a huge advantage as they had made enough preparation prior to its launching while others are caught in the trap without preparation.[16]

Highlighting this area of regulation, Yash Pal Committee report has dealt it sincerely in the report. The globalization may add to the exposure in the Indian higher education system, but it is also a worrying issue. Before taking any decision, we have to be very clear about the purpose it is going to achieve. Don't we want the best

16. Mithilesh Kumar Singh, "Challenges of Globalization on Indian Higher Education", Apeejay-Stya Education Research Foundation, New Delhi

learning experience to be shared by our students? If so, can this not be done by opening our doors to foreign scholar and making our rules more flexible? Interaction with the best minds of the world would only enhance the quality of our universities. But giving an open license to all and sundry carrying a foreign ownership tag to function like universities in India, most of them not even known in their countries would only help them earn profit for their parent institutions located outside or accrue profit to the shareholders. If the best of the foreign universities, say amongst the top 200 in the world, want to come here and work, they should be welcomed. Any decision in this regard has to be taken with utmost care keeping in mind the features, which are essential for an institution to be called a university. Such institutions should give an Indian degree and be subject to all the rules and regulations that would apply to any Indian university.[17]

Even in modern times every university carries some foreign engagements and entitlements. The international student exchange programmes, study abroad programmes and other such programmes are to be well regulated.

The foregoing debate and the concerns highlighted in the Yash Pal Committee Report clearly articulate the need of the regulatory mechanism for making education all inclusive.

Review of Literature

The Economic Times (2003)[18] writes that AICTE which works also through its state level units has been unresponsive or failed to check the mushrooming of ill standards institutes in the field of technical

17. Government of India (2008), *"Report of 'The Committee to Advise on Renovation and Rejuvenation of Higher Education", department of Higher Education, Ministry of Human Resource Development, New Delhi.*
18. The Economic Times (2003e), "New engineering colleges fail to meet AICTE norms," 25th May, New Delhi

education. It has happened many times that the institutes which were approved by the AICTE later it came to light that the institutes lacked on many ground as specified in the approval criteria of the Council. It further adds that according to a report of the Comptroller and Auditor General of India, each of the 171 new institutions that were audited failed on one or more pre-requisites of the AICTE.

Dahlman and Utz (2004)[19] study the growth pattern of Indian Economy and looks forward to how the transition to make it a knowledge economy—an economy that creates disseminates, and uses knowledge to enhance its growth and development, can be realized. He further debates on the nature of knowledge economy. He is of the view that the knowledge economy is often taken to mean only high-technology industries or information and communication technologies (ICTs). But it would be more appropriate, however, to use the concept more broadly to cover how any economy harnesses and uses new and existing knowledge to improve the productivity of agriculture, industry, and services and increase overall welfare. He signifies the importance of education in India's growth pattern.

Pawan Agarwal (2006)[20] opines that the structure and service delivery of higher education in India is changing and the challenges of expansion and diversification have become the major areas of concerns for the regulatory mechanism concerning higher education. The writer also highlights some other important areas of regulation; quality assurance, affordability, accountability and public-private partnership. Besides this he has analyzed the present system of regulation for higher

---

19. Carl Dahlman and Anuja Utz (2004),"India and the Knowledge Economy: Leveraging Strengths and Opportunities", Finance and Private Sector Development Unit of the World Bank's South Asia Region and The World Bank Institute.
20. Pawan Aggarwal (2006),"Higher Education in India; The Need for Change", working paper no.108,Indian Council for Research on International Economic Relations, New Delhi

education and has discussed the regulatory bodies like UGC and AICTE. The writer has also expressed the need to bring reform in the present regulatory mechanism for higher education.

Irena and Birute (2006)[21] analyses the role of higher education to economic development by highlighting private and societal benefits of university education as well as trying to look at possible negative effects that higher education expansion might have. He further develops how the higher education system and its application are helpful in facilitating development and particularly economic development as he reveals that a competitive economy can only be based on a well-educated population as well as a dynamic R&D sector. The two components of knowledge the human beings ("human capital") and the technology have become central to economic development. In the age of globalization, the knowledge economy discourse has become a way to characterize the new relationships between the state, society and economy and rendered higher education increasingly important for the international competitiveness of the nation states through their central tasks of generation, application and dissemination of knowledge and training high skilled labour force.

The Economic Times (2008)[22] reports that the AICTE has worked to have uniform fee structure for all the institutes of technical education in the country. It further writes that in 2008 the council initiated the process of setting guidelines on uniform fee structure for technical education across the country, responding to appeals made by the Consortium of Self-Financed Professional, Arts and Sciences Colleges in Tamil Nadu.

---

21. Irena Macerinskiene, Birute Vaiksnoraite (2006), "The Role OF Higher Education to Economic Development", VADYBA / MANAGEMEN, Volume 2, No.11, www.leidykla.eu/fileadmin/Vadyba/11/Irena_Macerinskiene_Birute_Vaiksnoraite.pdf
22. The Economic Times (2008a), "AICTE to come out with guidelines on uniform fee structure", 1st June, New Delhi

The Economic Times (2008)[23] have criticized the AICTE as it was observed that the council was involved in the unfair practices when it comes to provide approval to the institutes. While AICTE is known to have approved institutions with dubious antecedents, it has not recognized some of India's premier institutes like Indian School of Business (ISB), Hyderabad, and SP Jain, Mumbai.

The Economic Times (2008)[24] highlighted AICTE's inefficiency in having a healthy relationship between the industry and technical education which can otherwise be a link to the employability of students. It further adds the findings of a Parliamentary Committee and writes that Despite several initiatives taken for meaningful interaction between industry and academia for mutual benefits specific to technical education system, linkages between industry and technical institutions continue to remain weak.

Government of India (2008)[25] in Report of "The Committee to Advise Renovation and Rejuvenation of Higher Education" debates that the multiplicity of regulatory bodies in the field of higher education made regulation in the field of higher education more unmanageable and therefore proposes for a single National Level Commission, known as National Commission for Higher Education and Research (NCHER). It rightly brings out the flaws in the regulatory mechanism and also discusses the various challenges it has to face. The Report quotes, "Given the national aspiration for greater and equitable access to knowledge it is essential that the regulatory systems propel the

---

23. The Economic Times (2008b), "AICTE comes under Government scrutiny", 31st January, New Delhi
24. The Economic Times (2008c), "Concern over employability of tech students: Panel", 14th December, New Delhi
25. Government of India (2008), *"Report of 'The Committee to Advise on Renovation and Rejuvenation of Higher Education", department of Higher Education, Ministry of Human Resource Development, New Delhi.*

growth in the right direction. A well-designed regulatory system will also help to promote a high degree of professionalism in managing higher education institutions.

Government of India (2009)[26] in its 'Report to the Nation (2006-09)' also carries forward the debate on the regulatory mechanism in the field of higher education and also proposes one Independent National Level Regulatory Authority. In its report it has revealed how the regulatory bodies like UGC and AICTE has not been able to perform their assumed roles. It has also touched the main concerns of higher education system namely; Quality, Accountability, Accreditation, Financing, Access, Expansion and Diversification.

Hisham and Abdel (2009)[27] opine that higher education system is complementary to the economic development of a country and education is considered one of the most important aspects of the development of human resources. Education can be considered as one of the aspects of high productive investments, and this comply to several kinds of education, that is most of the economists realize the importance of education in the economic development, as they believe that machines and equipments are not as much important as men who create these machines, support them technically, and improve their productivity. So, machines will not be beneficial if knowledge and their required operating crews were not setup, and therefore, the investment would not be considered productive.

26. Government of India (2009), "National Knowledge Commission: Report to the Nation", National Knowledge Commission, New Delhi
27. Hisham Al-Smadi, Abdel Salam Njadat (2009), "The Role of Higher Education in the Economic Development of the Hashemite Kingdom of Jordan" Euro Journals Publishing, Inc. 2009,www.eurojournals.com/mefe_3_01.pdf

Akshat Mehta (2009)[28] opines that the regulatory governance has become one of the emerging areas of public administration. He further states that the state is more expected to play the role of regulator in today's world. He adds that the opening of the economy which has opened the gate for privatization in mostly public-sector occupied economy has been a challenging area for the regulatory mechanism in India.

AICTE (2009)[29] in its annual reports highlights the activities of AICTE and has comprehensively dealt with all major areas on which the Council regulates. The reports, approval procedure has provided knowledge to all the major policies and programmes of the Council, through which it performs its major functions, besides providing data. The report states that in order to promote research the Council the Council operates three schemes, namely, Modernization and Removal of Obsolescence (MODROBS), Research Promotion Scheme (RPS) and Nationally Coordinated Projects (NCP). A total of 544 Projects were approved for financial support under MODROBS and RPS schemes during the year 2008-2009 and the Council released a total amount of Rs.3594.07 Lakh. It further adds that there are several schemes for faculty development, namely, Quality Improvement Programme (QIP), Career Award for Young Teachers (CAYT), Emeritus Fellowship, Visiting Professorship, Seminar Grant, Travel Grant, Staff Development Programme, National Doctoral Fellowship, AICTE-INAE Distinguished Visiting Professorship and Financial Assistance to Professional Societies/ Bodies.

---

28. Akshat Mehta (2009), *Regulatory Governance In The Deregulated Telecom Sector: An Assessment of the Role of Telecom Regulatory Authority of India (PH.D Thesis)*, Department of Public Administration, Panjab University, Chandigarh (India).
29. All India Council for Technical Education (2008-09 a.), Annual Report 2008-09, New Delhi

MCI (2010)[30] in its annual reports specify all the area of regulation starting from providing approval to new institutes to maintaining Indian medical registrar, reports of its inspection activities, various rules and regulation, maintenance of medical ethics, governing teaching standard and other various areas of regulation. It comprehensively provides for the composition, organization and functions of the Council. The report adds that The Council carries out the inspection of medical colleges both at Undergraduate level and Post-Graduate level. The council carries out four kind of inspection; inspection for starting of medical college, inspection for starting Post-Graduate course in an already existing medical college, inspection for recognition of MBBS or Post-Graduate qualification, inspection for increase of seats in a particular course as per provision of Section 10A for continuance of recognition of qualification. The reports further provides the statistical date about the maintenance of Indian Medical Registrar and states that total number of doctors registered in the Country up to 31st March 2010 are 7, 97,764.

UGC (2010)[31] through its annual reports describes the various activities of University Grants Commission and writes that the Commission has been worked as a body regulating all the facets of higher education in India; starting from devising the admission procedure to allocation of funds and Grants-in-aid to the higher education institutes, promotion of excellence, research and development in all the areas of higher education through Commission's various schemes, maintenance of academic standards, development of various schemes for promotion of quality teaching, check on the mushrooming of sub-standard institutes, conducting relevant studies in higher education system, working for the social equity in higher education through the schemes

30. Medical Council of India (2009-10 a.), Annual Report, 2009-10, New Delhi
31. University Grants Commission (2008-09 a.), Annual Report 2008-09, New Delhi

etc. The reports also provide a relevant data on all these schemes. The report explains the various schemes for improving the teaching.

Mithilesh Kumar[32] has discussed an important aspect of higher education and that is globalization. The writer has explored the option of globalization and has brought out the pros and cons of the globalization aspect of higher education and has expressed his views that how it is going to affect our higher education system. He further adds that it is assumed that globalization promises dramatic and rewarding change to their education system, of societies which are relatively stable in their political, social and institutional makeup, while for others it may threaten the very stability needed to build well performing higher education system. It is also true, that so far globalization has given the advanced economies a huge advantage as they had made enough preparation prior to its launching while others are caught in the trap without preparation.

Times of India (2012)[33] reports how the AICTE from time to time take cognizance of the expansion of technical education and provides the data for the approval of new institutes. The addition to the existing infrastructure and rejecting the approval is the main area of concern of AICTE and it does it through the inspection. In the recent venture of its approval process, in April 2012, in order to expedite the admission process for professional courses, the council approved 102 new colleges of technical education

Times of India (2012)[34] writes how the AICTE works to promote the standard of technical education in India through its medium of

32. Mithilesh Kumar Singh, "Challenges of Globalization on Indian Higher Education", Apeejay-Stya Education Research Foundation, New Delhi
33. Times of India (2012a), "All India Council for Technical Education gives nod to 102 college" 18th April, New Delhi
34. Times of India (2012b), "AICTE cancels nod to 5 engineering colleges" 21st April, 2012, New Delhi

providing approval or rejecting the proposal of approval to the institutes in accordance to its described criteria. The council has been responsive in the case of those institutions involved in ill practices and has rejected their approval. In one of its recent move, in April 2012, in a bid to crack down on corruption in technical education institutes, the All India Council for Technical Education (AICTE) has cancelled recognition of five engineering colleges affiliated to Rajasthan Technical University (RTU) on grounds of their involvement in malpractices.

Times of India (2012)[35] reports that the AICTE through its medium of inspection works to check the maintenance of standards of institutes in technical education and takes notice of the developments taking place in the institutes. In its recent initiatives the council started carrying inspection of those institutions which were seeking increase in the seats of various courses of management and engineering. Conventionally, the colleges apply for hike in intake of seats on the web portal of AICTE furnishing details of the infrastructure, staff and students online. The applications are scrutinized online and permission given for additional seats. However, following complaints that many colleges do not have infrastructure and human resource that match the details provided in the online application, the AICTE decided to carry out surprise raids. In the past three years, many colleges are reported to have indulged in malpractices including lying about infrastructure and human resource. AICTE warned that colleges which are found flouting norms or providing incorrect information will be penalized.

Times of India (2012)[36]reports that the AICTE entertains the various demands of the states in lieu to the expansion of technical education and works in cooperative manner with the states. In March

35. Times of India (2012c), "AICTE raids colleges to verify online claims" 11th April, 2012, New Delhi
36. Times of India (2012d), "AICTE may bar new engineering, management colleges from 2014", March 14, New Delhi

2012, Several State Governments had requested AICTE not to clear the applications for starting new engineering colleges. They have cited the incidence of growing number of vacant BE/BTech seats in the existing colleges. So the council has taken a decision not to sanction approval for new applicants from 2013-14 for these states.

Times of India (2012)[37] reports that the inspection activities of the MCI which are intended to maintain the standards of medical education have become formality as institutes which lacked on the required standards also got approval from the Council. It further adds that MCI does not have enough qualified inspectors as of now to conduct strict and long duration inspections.

Times of India (2012)[38] brings about the criticism carried out by the reality show "Satyamev Jayate" and also reveals the cases of exploitation of medical ethics for example the show has brought out a real case of a person who met with an accident near Electronics City, located on the outskirts of Bangalore. It further states the ignorance and unresponsiveness of Medical Council to these cases.

Times of India (2012)[39] reports that the MCI has been inefficiently working and has not performed well as the regulation in the field of medical education is concerned. It states the findings of the task force of the Union Health Ministry which has decided to scrap all regulatory bodies, including the Medical Council of India, Dental Council of India, Pharmacy Council and the Nursing Council. It further adds that due to the inefficiency of MCI, it has drawn criticism from all sections of society and got judicial censure on several occasions.

---

37. Times of India(2012e), "Medical Council of India not very strict in holding the recognition inspection", June 14, New Delhi
38. Times of India (2012f), "Shaming the Hippocratic Oath", June 4, New Delhi.
39. Times of India (2009g), "MCI scrapped, single council for medical education", August 28, New Delhi.

The Economic Times (2012)[40] reports that the AICTE has been so far working as a promoter of research and development in the field of technical education and over the time it has been involved in the various collaborations to perform this role. In one of its recent initiative, Adding value to government's skill development initiative, the AICTE roped in Tata Institute of Social Sciences (TISS) to conduct studies on skill requirements and develop content for various sectors. **The Hindu (2012)**[41] reports that the MCI has been involved in the cases of corruption. It has also criticized MCI's Board of Governors for its alleged role in the malpractices and brings out the criticism carried out in the Parliament by the various M.P.s

Inferences Drawn from the Literature Reviewed

i. The main area of regulation by the different regulatory bodies in the field of higher education has been mainly the service delivery aspect of the higher education system.

ii. The present regulatory mechanism for higher education in India has been criticized for the multiplicity of regulatory bodies for each specific area.

iii. The regulatory mechanism in India is going through transition as the criticism of the present regulatory mechanism has led to the emerging of consensus for one single National Level Commission, encompassing all the regulatory bodies and for which the Bill is pending in the Parliament.

Significance of the Study

The higher education has been regarded as a medium facilitating development. So it becomes the major area of concern for any state,

40. The Economic Times(2012a), "AICTE signs MoU with TISS on skill development", 27th March, New Delhi.
41. The Hindu (2012a). "Lok Sabha passes MCI Board extension Bill despite Trinamool saying 'no'", May 7, New Delhi

pledging for the development and regulation of higher education thus becomes the most important subject on which every state wishes to ponder upon. Regulation in higher education has become more challenging with the arising challenges of commercialization, privatization and globalization. The present scenario of regulatory mechanism in India reveals that there is a debate being carried out to change the multiplicity of regulatory bodies with one Independent National Level Regulatory Commission in the field of higher education. In this regard it becomes important to comprehensively analyze some of the important regulatory bodies working in the field of higher education and to assess their performance and to make recommendations accordingly.

Objectives of the Study

The objectives of the study are to:

i. Study the working of University Grants Commission(UGC), and evaluating the role UGC as a regulator

ii. Describe the working of All India Council for Technical Education(AICTE), and evaluating the role AICTE as a regulator

iii. Study the working of Medical Council of India(MCI), and evaluating the role MCI as a regulator

iv. Recommend policy prescription for improving effectiveness of regulatory bodies.

v. To analyze the recommendation of various reports in lieu of National Commission for Higher Education in relation to the existing system of regulation.

Research Methodology

The study is based on secondary data. Secondary data has been collected from the sources such as annual reports of UGC, AICTE,

MCI, National Knowledge Commission, Report of 'The Committee to Advise on Renovation and Rejuvenation of Higher Education' popularly known as Yash Pal Committee Report, Five Year Plans, publications, newspapers, research journals, articles, various other reports and doctoral studys. Secondary data has also been collected through the vast resources of World Wide Web.

Chapterisation

The study has been organized into five chapters, namely:

1. Introduction
2. University Grants Commission (UGC) as a Regulator; introduction, Structure, Functioning and Evaluation of the Role
3. All India Council for Technical Education(AICTE); Emergence, Structure, Functioning and It's Evaluation
4. Medical Council of India(MCI) as a Regulator; introduction, Organization, Functioning and its assessment
5. Conclusion and Suggestions.

2

University Grants Commission (U.G.C) as a Regulator: Introduction, Structure, Functioning and Evaluation of the Role

The University Grants Commission (U.G.C.) has been the nodal agency and first of its kind in India, as the regulation in the field of higher education is concerned. The UGC was formally established in November 1956 as a statutory body of the Government of India through an Act of Parliament (The UGC Act, 1956) for the coordination, determination and maintenance of standards of university education in India. It monitors developments in the field of collegiate and university education and disburse grants to the universities and colleges. This chapter is divided into two parts; the first part comprehensively deals with the emergence of the UGC, its composition, organization, powers and functions and the second part is devoted to the assessment of UGC's role as a regulator in the field of higher education.

PART I

Inception of UGU, its Composition, Organization and Powers and Functions

University Grants Commission

The regulatory mechanism in higher education was formally introduced with the setting up of the University Grants Commission (U.G.C.) in 1956 under the UGC Act, 1956 of the Parliament. It was not a sudden realization of the fact that India needed a regulatory framework for its higher education system, the thought developed over the period of time due to the emerging challenges of expansion, access, quality assurance and lack of an institutionalized set up in this area. The first attempt to formulate a national system of education in India came in 1944 with the Report of the Central Advisory Board of Education on Post War Educational Development in India, also known as the Sargeant Report. It recommended the formation of a University Grants Committee, which was formed in 1945 to oversee the work of the three Central Universities of Aligarh, Banaras and Delhi. In 1947, the Committee was entrusted with the responsibility of dealing with all the then existing Universities. Soon after Independence, the University Education Commission was set up in 1948 under the Chairmanship of Dr. S Radhakrishnan "to report on Indian university education and suggest improvements and extensions that might be desirable to suit the present and future needs and aspirations of the country". It recommended that the University Grants Committee be reconstituted on the general model of the University Grants Commission of the United Kingdom with a full-time Chairman and other members to be appointed from amongst educationists of repute.[42]

In 1952, the Union Government decided that all cases pertaining to the allocation of grants-in-aid from public funds to the Central Universities and other Universities and institutions of higher learning might be referred to the University Grants Commission. Consequently, the University Grants Commission (UGC) was formally inaugurated by late Shri Maulana Abul Kalam Azad, the then Minister of Education, Natural Resources and Scientific Research on 28 December 1953. The UGC, however, was formally established only in November 1956 as a statutory body of the Government of India through an Act of Parliament for the coordination, determination and

42. http://en.wikipedia.org/wiki/University_Grants_Commission_(India)

maintenance of standards of university education in India. In order to ensure effective region-wise coverage throughout the country, the UGC has decentralized its operations by setting up six regional centres at Pune, Hyderabad, Kolkata, Bhopal, Guwahati and Bangalore. The head office of the UGC is located at Bahadur Shah Zafar Marg in New Delhi, with two additional bureaus operating from 35, Feroze Shah Road and the South Campus of University of Delhi as well.[43]

However the scope of University Grants Commission's activities has experienced a broadened change over the time as it was entrusted with more functions and activities. The overall and major function of UGC at the time of its constitution was only pertaining to the allocation of grants-in-aids to the universities from the public funds but later on it was endowed with function by which it supervises almost all administrative and educational facets of higher education institutions.

The UGC's mandate includes

1. Promoting and coordinating university education.
2. Determining and maintaining standards of teaching, examination and research in universities.
3. Framing regulations on minimum standards of education.
4. Monitoring developments in the field of collegiate and university education; disbursing grants to the universities and colleges.
5. Serving as a vital link between the Union and state governments and institutions of higher learning.

Advising the Central and State governments on the measures necessary for improvement of university education.[44]

---

43. www.ugc.ac.in/about/genesis.html , the website of University Grants Commission
44. www.ugc.ac.in/about/mandate.html, the website of University Grants Commission

Composition

The University Grant Commission consist of –

1. Chairman,
2. Vice-Chairman, and
3. Ten other members, to be appointed by the Central Government.

The Chairman is chosen from among persons who are not officers of the Central Government or of any State Government.

The eligibility criteria of selection of other members which are included in clause (3) is discussed below-

a. Two members are from among the officers of the Central Government, to represent the Central Government;

b. the other four members are chosen from among persons who, at the time of selection are the teachers of Universities; and

c. The remaining members are chosen from among the following persons-

   i. Who have knowledge of, or experience in, Agriculture, Commerce, Forestry or Industry;

   ii. Who are members of the engineering, legal, medical or any other learned profession; or

   iii. Who are Vice-Chancellors of Universities or who, not being teachers of Universities, are in the opinion of the Central Government, educationists of repute or have obtained high academic distinctions.

Provided that not less than one-half of the numbers chosen under this clause shall be from among persons who are not officers of the Central Government or of any State Government.

The Vice-Chairman exercises such powers, and discharges such of the duties, of the chairman as may be prescribed. Every appointment under this section takes effect from the date on which it is notified by the central government in the official gazette.

The UGC Act provides for the term of five years for the chairman, three years for the vice-chairman and members or until they attain the age of sixty-five years, whichever is earlier. The Commission meets at such times and places and observes such rules of procedure in regard to the transaction of business at its meetings as may be provided by regulations made under The UGC Act.[45]

Organization of the Commission

The Commission had so far been administering its working through a centralized set up till late 1970s. But due to the emerging challenges of expansion and diversification taking place in the area of higher education, it seemed that the existing institutionalized set up was insufficient to cater the emerging needs and to deal with these challenges. To make the Commission more efficient in achieving its target was also the reason that inspired the Commission to look after the alternatives. As a solution the Commission thought of decentralizing its working, through some divisions like regional centers, inter university centers and academic staff college. Some of these initiatives came in the wake of national policy on education 1986. Presently the Commission has the following division:

1. UGC Regional Offices

In pursuance to the National Policy on Education (1986), the UGC decentralized its working by opening seven regional offices (earlier were six) catering to the states under it. The objectives of setting up these offices were to bring about decentralization and to ensure that a large number of colleges through the country, which are covered under the UGC Act, will have better opportunities of response to their needs and problems by way of easier access.

45. www.ugc.ac.in/policy/ugc_act.pdf, the website of University Grants Commission

The details of the regional office viz. the States assigned to each regional office are given below :

a. Southern Eastern Regional Office (SERO)
Location: Hyderabad
Date of Establishment: 20.09.1994
Total number of Colleges: 668
States Covered: Andhra Pradesh, Pondicherry, Andaman & Nicobar and Tamil Nadu

b. Western Regional Office (WRO)
Location: Pune
Date of Establishment: 11.11.1994
Total number of Colleges: 996
States Covered: Maharashtra, Gujarat, Goa, Dadar & Nagar Haveli, Daman and Deu

c. Central Regional Office (CRO)
Location: Bhopal
Date of Establishment: 01.12.1994
Total number of Colleges: 791
States Covered: Madhya Pradesh, Chhattisgarh and Rajasthan

d. Northern Regional College Bureau (NRCB)
Location: Delhi
Total number of Colleges: 922
States Covered: Jammu & Kashmir, Himachal Pradesh, Punjab, Chandigarh, Haryana, Delhi, Uttar Pradesh and Uttrakhand

e. North-Eastern Regional Office (NERO)
Location: Guwahati
Date of Establishment: 01.04.1995
Total number of Colleges: 253
States Covered: Assam, Meghalaya, Mizoram, Manipur, Tripura, Arunachal Pradesh and Nagaland

f. Eastern Regional Office (ERO)
Location: Kolkata
Date of Establishment: 03.09.1996
Total number of Colleges: 1009
States Covered: West Bengal, Bihar, Jharkhand, Orissa and Sikkim

g. South-Western Regional Office (SWRO)
Location: Bangalore
Date of Establishment: 25.04.1999
Total number of Colleges: 714
States Covered: Kerala, Karnataka and Lakshadweep

2. Inter-University Centers:

The UGC has been setting up autonomous centres, from 1984 onwards. The rationale behind having Inter-Universities Centre as the part of UGC's structure was to provide common facilities for research and for various services and programmes to the universities as it was not possible for an individual institution to obtain these facilities. A brief introduction of the inter-university centers, established by UGC is given below:

a. Inter University Accelerator Centre (IUAC): Inter University Accelerator Centre, situated at New Delhi was the first Inter-University Centre to be established by the UGC in 1984. The objective of this particular IUC is to promote group research programmes, collaborating universities, IITs and other institution of higher education. The centre was also aimed at developing world class facilities in institution of higher education for research or accelerator based research. It also works to promote group activities and human research development in experimental science and other branches of knowledge.

b. Inter University centre for Astronomy and Astro-Physics (IUCAA): IUCAA, Pune came into existence in 1988 as an autonomous centre of excellence, working especially in the field of Astronomy and Astro-Physics. It looked after the promotion of the growth and development of research activities in Astronomy and Astro-Physics in institution of higher education. IUCAA focused itself in providing centralized facilities for subjects not adequately covered in the university departments and colleges.

c. UGC-DAE Consortium for Scientific Research: UGC-DAE was created in the year 1990 for promoting competence and excellence in research in important areas of science and technology in higher education system. The centre works to facilitate and provide the institutional mechanism for the optimum use of major research facilities established by the department of Atomic Energy such as Dhruv Reactor of Mumbai, Variable Energy Cyclotron Centre (VECC) at Kolkata and Synchrotron Radiation Sources at Indore. The facilities of IUC can be availed by scientists from any university.

d. Consortium for Education Communication (CEC): Consortium of Educational Communication, New Delhi, employs media communication to cater to the needs of higher education in the country. Educational programmes are produced by Educational Media Research Centres (EMRCs) and Audio Visual Research Centres (AVRCs) located at various higher educational institutes in the country. These programmes are telecast on Doordarshan and Gyandarshan Channels.

e. **Information and Library Network (INFLIBNET):** This particular IUC was brought to the structure of UGC as a network of libraries that looked to develop various facilities in the library network. It promotes the modernization of libraries, serves as Information Centre for transfer and access of information, supports scholarships and learning and academic pursuits through a National Network of Libraries in around 264 Universities, Colleges and R &D Institutions across the country.

f. **Inter University Center for International Studies (IUC-IS):** The UGC has established Inter-University Centres (IUCs) at Osmania University, Hyderabad. It aims to provide equipment and facilities to the researchers of different universities. Firstly the facilities provided by this IUC were only for the researchers who were in the field of science and technology but now the provision is there for another IUC of this kind, which provides its services to the researches in the field of Humanities and Social Science by taking over academic and physical infrastructure available at Indo-American Centre for International Studies. The proposed IUC would be providing dynamic and vibrant platform for academicians from India, SAARC region, Central Asian and other countries. The main objective of the IUC would be to address contemporary development issues with multi disciplinary approach in the following areas.

   i. Education, Commerce, Economics of development of these countries along with the interface with the developed countries.

   ii. World trade, GATS, IPR, financial management for international understanding.

   iii. Conflict management, diplomacy, development and peace initiatives between various countries.

   iv. Human rights, human values, life skills and learning to live together.

   v. Art, literature and other allied areas.

h. **National Assessment and Accreditation Council (NAAC):** UGC's main areas of regulation are; evaluating the performance of universities, their assessment and most importantly providing accreditation to the institutions. The Commission has a separate body to deal with these complex tasks, which is known as a National Assessment and Accreditation Council (NAAC).

NAAC was established by the UGC in September 1994 at Bangalore for evaluating the performance of the Universities and Colleges in the Country. NAAC's mandate includes the task of performance evaluation, assessment and accreditation of universities and colleges in the country. The philosophy of NAAC is based on objective and continuous improvement rather than being punitive or judgmental, so that all institutions of higher learning are empowered to maximize their resources, opportunities and capabilities. Assessment is a performance evaluation of an institution and /or its units and is accomplished through a process based on self-study and peer review using defined criteria. Accreditation refers to the certification given by NAAC which is valid for a period of five years. At present the Assessment and Accreditation by NAAC is done on a voluntary basis.

3. National Facilities Centre

The UGC has established 4 National Facilities Centre in the selected universities as per details given below:-

i. Western Regional Instrumentation Centre, Mumbai, Mumbai University

ii. M.S.T. Radar Facilities, Sri Venkateshwar University, Tirupati

iii. Inter University Centre for Humanities and Social Sciences IUCHSS, Indian Institute of Advanced Study, Shimla

iv. Crystal Growth Centre, Anna University, Madras.

4. Academic Staff Colleges (ACS):

One of the major part of UGC's structure is Academic Staff College through which the Commission has facilitated itself in organizing various course for the teaching community in order to help them to be familiar with the latest developments in their disciplines. All over India 45 academic staff colleges were created by the UGC as a place where special short-term courses could be run for serving teachers from institutions of higher education. The ASC provides mainly two types of course:

(a) **The Refresher Course**: The refreshes course is aimed at exposing teachers to the latest developments in their respective disciplines.

(b) **The Orientation Course**: The Orientation Course is especially for the new teachers. It seeks to introduce the freshly recruited teacher to the challenging vocation of teaching in today's India.

The ASC conducts around 20 such one month courses every year in its vicinities, with two courses usually being conducted simultaneously. The courses offered are on a wide variety of disciplines ranging from History, Political Science, Sociology, Economics and International Relations to Life Sciences, Environmental Sciences, Physics, Biotechnology, Computer Science and foreign languages.[46]

Powers and Functions of the Commission

The UGC was formally established in November 1956 as a statutory body of the Government of India through an Act of Parliament for the coordination, determination and maintenance of standards of university education in India. However the scope of University Grants commission's activities has experienced a broadened change over the time as it was entrusted with more functions and activities. The overall and major function of UGC at the time of its constitution was only pertaining to the allocation of grants-in-aids to the universities from the public funds but later on it was endowed with function by which it supervises almost all administrative functions of higher education institutions. The brief analysis of the functions of Commission is as followed:

46. www.ugc.ac.in/orgn/commision.html, the website of University Grants Commission

1. The general duty of the commission, as described in the UGC Act is to take all such steps as it may think fit for the promotion and co-ordination of university education and for the determination and maintenance of standards of teaching, examination and research in universities. The Commission takes all these steps after consulting the universities or other bodies concerned. And for the purpose of performing its functions under this, the commission:

    a. Inquire into the financial needs of Universities;

    b. To allocate and disburse funds and grants, out of the Fund of the Commission to Universities established or incorporated by or under a Central Act, for the maintenance and development of such Universities or for any other general or specified purpose;

    c. Allocate and disburse, out of the fund of the Commission, such grants to other universities as it may deem necessary or appropriate for the development of such universities or for the maintenance, or development, or both, of any specified activities of such universities or for any other general or specified purpose: provided that in making any grant to any such university, the Commission shall give due consideration to the development of the university concerned, its financial needs, the standard attained by it and the national purposes which it may serve,

    d. Recommend to any university the measures necessary for the improvement of University education and advice the university upon the action to be taken for the purpose of implementing such recommendation;

    e. To advise the central government or any state government on the allocation of any grants to Universities for any general or specified purpose out of the consolidated fund of India or the Consolidated fund of the state, as the case may be;

f. To advise any authority, if such advice is asked for, on the establishment of a new university or on proposals connected with the expansion of the activities of any University;

g. To advise the Central Government or any State Government or university on any question, which may be referred to the commission by the Central Government or the State Government or the university, as the case may be?

h. To collect information on all such matters relating to university education in India and other countries as it thinks fit and make the same available to any university;

i. It may ask a university to furnish it with such information as may be needed relating to the financial position of the university or the studies in the various branches of learning undertaken in that university, together with all the rules and regulations relating to the standards of teaching and examination in that university respecting each of such branches of learning;

j. Perform such other functions as may be prescribed or as may be deemed necessary by the commission for advancing the cause of higher education in India or as may be incidental or conducive to the discharge of the above functions.

2. The Commission also undertakes the regulation of fees and prohibition of donation in certain cases. It does the regulation of fees by fixing up the fees and the scales of fees through consultation with the concerned university and universities

3. One of the important functions of the Commission is carrying out the inspection activities of the universities in regards to

funding of the concerned universities. And it has the power to reject any grant to a university not declared fit by the Commission to receive such grant after the inspection of the concerned university.

4. The Commission has the responsibility to prepare its budget in respect of the financial year, showing the estimated receipts and expenditure, and copies of this will be forwarded to the Central Government. The commission also represents its budget in its annual reports in a comprehensive manner
5. The Commission has to prepare an annual report giving a true and full account of its activities during the previous year, and copies thereof are forwarded to the central government and the government causes the same to be laid before both houses of parliament.
6. The Commission has the responsibility to maintain such books of account and other books in relation to its account in such form and in such manner as may be prescribed, in consultation with the Comptroller and Auditor-General of India. The Commission as soon as may be after closing its annual accounts, prepares a statement of accounts in such form, and forwards the same to the comptroller and auditor-general by such date, as the central governments may, in consultation with the Comptroller and Auditor- General, determine.
7. The Commission furnishes to the central government such returns or other information with respect to its property or activities as the central government may, from time to time, require.

In the discharge of its functions under this Act, the Commission is guided by such directions on questions of policy relating to national purposes as may be given to it by the Central Government. If any dispute arises between the Central Government and the Commission as to whether a question is or is not a question of policy relating to national purposes, the decision of the Central Government is taken as final.[47]

Part II

Assessment of UGC as A Regulator in Higher Education

Assessment of UGC as a Regulator in Higher Education

National Knowledge Commission and Yash Pal Committee report on 'Renovation and Rejuvenation of Higher Education have preferred one central regulatory mechanism namely National Commission For Higher Education and Research (NCHER), instead of many regulatory bodies, and which is under process to become an important legislation in the field of regulation in higher education as the Bill is pending in the Parliament, it becomes relevant to discuss how this suggestive measures took place. Was there any weakness in the existing system of regulation, or was it the inefficiency of these regulatory bodies or too much interference and governance or over-regulation caused by this system was the reason behind this?

In this part of the chapter we will discuss the assessment of University Grants Commission, how it has fared so far, what were its major achievements and weaknesses, or the role it has played as a regulator.

The UGC, which was entrusted the tasks to look after the funding of universities, coordination, determination and maintenance of standards of universities in its initial emergence as directed in UGC Act 1956, its scope of activities got widened drastically over the period of time. At the time of Independence of India, there were only 20 Universities and 500 Colleges in the country. The numbers now are

47. http://www.ugc.ac.in/orgn/commision.html, the website of University Grants Commission

increased to 24 times in the case of the Universities, 52 times in the case of Colleges and the students enrolment has gone up to 49 times in the formal system of higher education in comparison to the figures at the time of Independence.[48]

The Commission which was constituted for a smaller numbers of institutes had to face many administrative, structural challenges in order to cater the emerging needs in the field of higher education. It has also decentralized its working to make itself more efficient. The task of providing financial assistance and the criterion for the selection, it's monitoring and evaluation is not that much easy, it need a well committed effort. Determination and maintenance of standards of universities is also a complex procedure.

In recent years, the Indian Higher Education System has become fully aware of the need for quality. Quality and excellence could not be attained overnight. Organized and focused efforts are needed to achieve this goal. The unplanned growth of higher education coupled with lack of resources affects the quality of education. A careful distribution of resources is mandatory to achieve quality and excellence along with access and equality. The UGC has taken upon itself this onerous task and has succeeded in maintaining the quality of education. It has launched many schemes, which have made some impact in the system viz.

1. Innovative Programmes including Emerging Areas
2. International Cooperation
3. Identification of Universities and Colleges with Potential for Excellence
4. Networking of Universities and Colleges
5. Faculty Improvement Programme

---

48. University Grants Commission (2008-09 a.), Annual Report 2008-09, New Delhi, pp. 18

6. National Eligibility Test (NET)
7. Schemes for strengthening of Research
8. Programmes for the development of Engineering and Technical Education
9. Programme for the Development of Management Education
10. Programme for the Development of Computer Education and Up gradation / Augmentation of Computer Facilities
11. Accreditation System[49]

However it will be more convenient, to firstly identify the areas of regulation of UGC, while assessing the commission. The assessment will mainly focus on the following aspects:

1. Allocation of funds and Grants-in-Aid to the Central Universities and Other Universities
2. Promotion of excellence in higher education
3. Promotion of qualitative research and teaching
4. Towards social equity and socio-economic mobility of the disadvantaged sections of the society
5. Inculcating marketing skills in the students
6. Promoting the relevance and value based education
7. Inclusion of ICT in higher education system
8. Regulating the studies conducted in the area of higher education
9. Dealing with the menace of existence and mushrooming of fake institutions in the field of higher education
10. Regulating the deemed universities and autonomous colleges.

Now we will briefly discuss the above mentioned area of regulation;

---

49. www.ugc.ac.in/policy/quality_assurance.html, website of University Grants Commission .

1. **Allocation of Funds and Grants-in-Aid to the Central Universities and Other Universities:** it is the traditional function of UGC, since its inception it was known as a body which looked after the overall funding of grants-in-aid and funds to the various central and other universities and institution of higher education. Over the period of time it has devised programmes, schemes and funding mechanism such as Special Assistant Programme (SAP), that caters to the different needs of these institutions

2. **Promotion of Excellence in Higher Education:** The UGC has been so far a promoter of excellence in higher education with an emphasis on quality in research and development through its initiatives. It has awarded those colleges and universities which are faring well on academic grounds through its schemes. It provides special financial assistance through special grants to the identified colleges and universities. This action and initiative of UGC does only inspire the identified universities to maintain its academic standards but also set standards for the other universities and college and motivate them to achieve the same academic standards. Under General Plan Development Assistance, the UGC assists each eligible University for the overall development covering the aspects namely, enhancing access, ensuring equity, imparting relevant education, improving quality and excellence, making their University administration more effective, providing more Faculty Improvement Programmes, enhancing facilities for students, augmenting research facilities and any other plans of the University. In order to fulfill these objectives, the financial assistance to meet the requirements of the University in terms of infrastructure, staff, equipment, books & journals, library etc. can be provided by the

UGC under the General Plan Development Grant during XI Plan period.[50]

In promotion of Excellence the various schemes of the UGC are as follow;

i. **College with Potential for Excellence:** In it scheme of "College with Potential for Excellence", it intends to identify about 100 colleges across the country and to support them to improve their academic infrastructure, adopt innovations in teaching methods, evaluation etc. During the first phase, 47 colleges were selected. Each of these colleges was sanctioned 50% of the allocated amount during 2004-2005. During second phase, out of 333 proposals recommended by 65 Universities, the Standing Committee selected 50 more colleges based on the revised scoring scale. During 2008-2009, an amount of Rs.12.33 crores had been released to the selected colleges. The proposals for filling up the slots have been invited during Phase-III from the Universities located in those states for which the quota fixed for CPE status is not exhausted during Phase I & II and these proposals are being evaluated by the Standing Committee for final selection. During XI Plan, 82 potential colleges are to be identified.[51]

ii. **Provision of Autonomous College:** This initiative of UGC has provided much needed freedom and flexibility in the higher education system as in order to provide academic freedom to those colleges which are working and performing well on the account of academic standards, UGC confers them the autonomous status. As on

50. University Grants Commission (2008-09 a.), Annual Report 2008-09, op. cit., pp.5
51. Ibid., pp.6

31.03.2009, autonomous status had so far been given to 314 Colleges spread over 58 universities of 16 states. The UGC Regional Offices released grants to the extent of Rs.28.76 crores to these autonomous colleges during 2008-09.[52]

iii. **Centre of Excellence and Universities with Potential for Excellence:** To achieve excellence in teaching and research, the UGC has been assisting identified universities for granting the status of "Universities with Potential for Excellence" and "Centre for Excellence". In the first phase, five universities were identified and granted the above mentioned status. In the second phase, 12 universities have been identified for establishing "Centre of Excellence" in the identified specialized areas. During Tenth Plan, four more universities were identified for according the status of "University with Potential for Excellence" against the target of five universities. Against the allocation of Rs.30 crores to each of the four universities, an amount of Rs.10 crores as seed grant was also released to each of the four universities during 2006-07. A total grant of Rs.20.00 crores had been paid to these Universities during 2008-09. During XI Plan, six more potential universities are to be identified. Accordingly, proposals from universities have been invited.[53]

iv. **Special Assistance Programme (SAP):** The UGC through its Special Assistance Programme (SAP) supports the university departments in Science including Bio-Science, Engineering and Technology, Humanities and Social Sciences for achieving excellence in research and

52. Ibid., pp.6
53. Ibid., pp.6

for improving the quality of post-graduate teaching programme. As on 31.03.2009, the number of SAP supported departments had been 723 as compared to 577 in the previous year. During the reporting year, as many as 145 departments had been inducted at DRS level. During 2008-09, the departments at various levels had been financially assisted to the extent of Rs.51.09 Crores. The UGC also provides the schemes like Assistance for Strengthening of Infrastructure for Science and Technology (ASIST) and Assistance for Strengthening of Infrastructure for humanities and Social Sciences (ASHISS), through which it provides grants to buy equipment for the research objectives which are not covered under SAP.[54]

v. **Bilateral Exchange programmes:** Bilateral Exchange Programmes has been one of the main programmes adding exposure to the initiatives of UGC in achieving excellence. The Bilateral Exchange programmes connected with Higher Education field have been in operation with 44 countries. During the reporting year, the UGC hosted the visits of 53 foreign scholars/delegates from various countries and deputed 90 Indian scholars abroad.[55]

3. **Promoting and Supporting Research:** UGC has a history of promoting, supporting and concentrating its activities on research and research projects in various disciplines of humanities, social sciences, physical and life sciences and through the medium of financial assistance it regulates the research activities. It has provisions of many programmes and schemes, in order to promote and support research activities, like of Research Project for Teachers, Emeritus Fellowship Scheme, and Junior Research Fellowship (JRF) etc. UGC undertakes the tasks of organizing

54. Ibid., pp.6
55. Ibid., pp.164

national-level seminars, conferences, workshops for bringing together experts from different parts of the country and abroad to share and exchange knowledge and ideas. It has the distinction of making its effort in order to equalize the disparities among the different strata of the society in the field of higher education and research as it provides special scholarships for the students who belong to SC/STs, OBC and minorities. UGC provides 2000 Rajiv Gandhi National Fellowships to SC/ST candidates (1333 for SC and 667 for ST) to undertake advanced studies and Research leading to M.Phil. /Ph.D. degrees. For minorities it provides Maulana Abul Kalam Azad Scholarship. The purpose of the scheme of PG Indira Gandhi Scholarship for Single Girl Child is to achieve and promote girls education by supporting through scholarships to such girls who happen to be the only child in their families and also providing an incentive for the parents to observe small family norms.[56]

4. **Promoting Social Equity In Higher Education:** UGC has taken initiatives through its various schemes and programmes that have attempted to facilitate social equity in higher education system. Its schemes have worked out on providing mechanism that promotes and facilitates the inclusion of disadvantaged section in the education system. Towards social equity and socio-economic mobility of the disadvantaged sections of the society, the UGC has been implementing coaching schemes for SC/ST/OBC (non-creamy layer/ Minorities viz. remedial coaching at UG & PG level, coaching scheme for entry in services and coaching scheme for preparing SC/ST/OBC/Minority candidates for NET/SET. Institutions having sufficient SC/ST/Minority Communities students are considered for financial assistance. General candidates with economically poor background may also be allowed for such

56. Ibid., pp.10-12

coaching classes. It also provides scholarships to the meritorious students in various disciplines at undergraduate level to pursue their PG, with the objective of promoting and nurturing the talented students.[57]

5. **Monitoring the Various Schemes:** The UGC's regulation in this above mentioned area is not only of formulating and providing provisions for the promotion of research but it also performs monitoring task in order to have a check on the implementation of these policies and programmes. For its every research funding programmes it evaluate the performance of research, annually or bi-annually, in order to check the output of the concerned person/agency's research and to insure itself that its funds and scholarships are being well utilized. For Example in the Case of JRF every research scholar has to submit his performance reports of research activities. To make colleges and universities more responsive to the needs and constraints of the disadvantaged social groups, the UGC had planned to establish Equal Opportunity Cell (EOC) in Colleges and Universities to oversee the effective implementation of policies and programmes for these groups and to provide guidance and counseling in academic, financial, social and other matters. One time grant of Rs.2.00 lakhs will be provided for establishing office of the EOC. The Standing Committee for welfare of Minorities has regularly been monitoring and reviewing the on-going scheme for Minorities.[58]

6. **Promoting Women Education and Development:** Women Education has been one of the major concerns of the UGC, as it has developed schemes in order to promote women education. The scheme of "Development of Women Studies" envisages

57. Ibid., pp.12-13
58. Ibid., pp.13

assistance to universities and colleges for setting up centres and cells for women studies to undertake research, develop curricula and organize training and extension work in the areas of gender equity, economic self-reliance of women, girls education, social and population issues etc. There were now 67 Women Studies Centres established in various Universities/ Colleges. The Expert Committee, which met on 05.03.2009, had recommended 46 more Women Studies Centres for establishment in universities and colleges. During 2008-09, an amount of Rs.3.10 crores had been released to the centres established prior to XI Plan. The specific objectives of the scheme of capacity building of Women Manager in Higher Education are to develop a perspective plan and strategy for reducing the gender gap in higher education system, to offer various training programmes at different levels for stimulating women to aspire to become administrators etc. At present, only three types of training and skill development workshops are being conducted. During 2008-09, one Training of Trainers and 79 Sensitization/Awareness/ Motivation Workshops had been organized by various universities and colleges and an amount of Rs.3.02 crores had been released to the institutions.[59]

7. **Promotion of Market Skills**: The another specific area of regulation is to promote the market skills in the students, to inculcate such knowledgeable experience in students which will be helpful for them in their future endeavors, when they will deal with the practicality of their subjects or when they will enter the markets. UGC ensures that the graduates who pass out after completing the career oriented courses, have knowledge, skills and aptitudes for gainful employment so as to reduce pressure on institutes of higher learning for Master degree. The UGC has been assisting institutions to the tune of Rs.7.00 lakhs

59. Ibid., pp.13

for Humanities and Commerce and Rs.10.00 lakhs for Science Streams as one time seed money for five years towards purchase of books and journals, lab and other equipment, remuneration to guest faculty etc. The Colleges/ Universities are required to opt for three courses only. During the reporting year, as many as 451 proposals of institutions had been approved for financial assistance. A total grant of Rs.42.29 crores had also been released to the Universities and Colleges during 2008-2009.[60]

8. **Relevance Based Education:** The Commission has been promoting the relevance and value based education. It has undertaken activities like establishing teaching-cum-research centres in universities called as Centres for study of Social Exclusion and Inclusion Policy. Its other initiatives like Adult, Continuing Education, Extension (ACEE) and Field outreach (FO), universities have been involved for organizing programmes such as Literacy, Post-Literacy, Continuing Education, Legal Literacy, Environment Education etc. involving students and teachers. The Commission has introduced such value based programmes like post-graduate degree, diploma and certificate courses as well as for holding seminars, symposia and workshops on Human Rights and Duties Education for spreading awareness among the teachers and students, the UGC has been providing financial assistance to various Universities and Colleges.[61]

9. **Introducing ICT:** Another important initiative of Commission is the introduction of information technology and computer application in the field of higher education. It not only involves introducing ICT as a subject in some of the discipline but also through its programme of INFONET Digital Library Consortium, it provides current as well as archival access to more than 5000 Core and peer-reviewed journals and 9

60. Ibid., pp.14
61. Ibid., pp.15

bibliographic databases from 23 publishers and aggregators in different disciplines.

The Commission, from time to time has taken initiative in order to improve the governance and efficiency of higher education system. Its major initiative includes reviving our tradition to support higher education, and to encourage the participation of society in the development of universities, the Commission has decided to continue the scheme entitled "Incentives for Resource Mobilization" during the XI Plan. The UGC has initiated e-governance of Higher Education and UGC Offices with an aim of improving information and service delivery, making managements accountable, transparent, less corruptive and effective. With a broad goal of attaining excellence in academic governance, the UGC has regularly been imparting training to the academic administrators of Universities/Colleges and UGC Officers. For this, guidelines have been prepared. During 2008-09, no training programmes for academic administrators of universities & colleges and UGC officers had been conducted and hence no expenditure had been incurred.[62]

10. **Conducting the Relevant Studies:** The University Grants Commission has a record of studies conducted in the area of higher education from time to time on the areas related to the field of higher education, and which has been quiet a helpful experience in policy formulation and determining new goals and objectives. It had sponsored a number of studies on various dimensions of higher education in the country in order to develop necessary information base as a source material to prepare a report on approach and strategy for the Eleventh Five Year Plan (2007-2012). The studies are related to expansion, inclusiveness, quality and finance. The information generated

62. Ibid., pp. 15

by these studies has been used for preparation of perspective of the XI Plan and the findings have helped in shaping its goals and objectives. The book entitled, "Higher Education in India" has been based on the studies sponsored by the UGC.[63]

The Commission has been entrusted one another important task. It is empowered under Section 12(h) of the UGC Act, 1956 to collect information on all such matters relating to University education in India and other countries as it thinks fit and under Section 12(i), it may require a University to furnish it with such information as may be needed relating to the financial position of the university or the studies in the various branches of learning undertaken in that university, together with all the rules and regulations relating to the standards of teaching and examination in that university respecting each of such branches of learning. It collection of data includes to review the numbers of universities, colleges working in the country, new enrollements in this field, showing their trends of increase and decrease and that too state wise. The Commission also collects data about the student enrollements in various courses at all level in universities/colleges and other institutions of higher education, faculty strength and also the no. of research degrees. In its women education centric data, commission works to have numerical analysis on the growth of enrollements of women in higher education, state wise, number of women colleges etc. These data are duly represented in the commission annual reports.

11. **Regulating the Deemed Universities and Dealing with the Menace of Existence and Mushrooming of Fake Institutions:** The Commission awards the status of deemed university and autonomous colleges to the universities and colleges which

63. Ibid., pp.1-3

under the review of UGC fulfils the criteria to be the same and have their academic standards well maintained and have sufficient infrastructural facilities. In the regard to the regulation of deemed university the recent work of the Commission comes under scan. On direction from the Central Government the UGC constituted an Expert committee under the chairmanship of Prof. B.S. Sonde to draft the Fee Regulations for Deemed Universities. The Committee started its work in August, 2007. The draft Regulations formulated by the Committee had been considered by the Commission in its meeting held on 10-11 December, 2008 and decided to review the Regulations with the help of another Expert Committee headed by Prof. Tareen, Commission Member. In the Commission meeting held on 22nd June, 2009, the final Regulations had been considered and approved by the Commission. These Regulations have already been sent to the Ministry on 26th June, 2009 for its concurrence.

The Commission has been entrusted with one more important responsibility to deal with the menace of existence and mushrooming of Fake Institutions and fake degrees/mark sheets in the country. To undertake this task the UGC has constituted Fake Universities Cell, which was set up on 30th May, 1996, and later on, it was renamed as Malpractices Cell. This cell collects information through print media and other sources and brings all cases / instances of the fake institutions to the notice of the Commission. The UGC in order to be more responsive to the advancements and challenges taking place in higher education field, it has taken positive steps with the introduction of some new cells to have regulatory mechanism for these advancements and challenges. This adds to the composition of commission; vigilance cell to check corruption effectively, sex harassment cell of women at work place, legal cell to cope up with the legal entitlements, desk to monitor and coordinate the replies of parliament question received, right to information act cell to provide information to the applicants under RTI Act, internal audit cell, pay scale cell, SC/ST/OBC cell, minority cell and the last one and one of the most active one specially these days is the ragging cell to check to menace of ragging and curb it.[64]

12. **Reviewing the Performance of Universities:** In the beginning of every five year plan period, the UGC reviews the performance of the Universities during the previous plan period and assesses the requirements of the universities for the next Plan. Accordingly, a Performa to evaluate the performance of the universities during the X Plan has been developed eliciting information on various aspects- academic, administrative and financial from the universities. On receipt of information with regard to both X Plan review as well as XI Plan requirements, the Visiting Committees visits the universities to assess the performance of the universities during X Plan period and requirements for the XI Plan.[65]

Assessing the role of the UGC, The Yash Pal committee report has praised the commission as it writes in the report that only a few organizations such as the UGC took major initiatives in fostering educational innovations such as setting up of inter-university centres to facilitate national synergy in research efforts among universities and to optimize the investments in sophisticated research infrastructure. The creation of country-wide educational communication facility through multiple platforms and creating large scale contents; the setting up of national network of libraries including e-journals for convenient access to higher educational institutions across the country; special incentives to advanced centres of research; and additional resources to institutions with potential for excellence were some of the other initiatives of the

64. Ibid., pp.16-25
65. www.ugc.ac.in/11plan/english11/UGC reviews.pdf, website of University Grants Commission.

UGC in the recent past. However the initiatives occurred randomly with no sustainable goals for further multiplications.[66]

Critical Evaluation

The UGC in its working has been facing criticism because of the failure in some of the arena of its assumed role. However the reports of Yash Pal Committee and National Knowledge Commission has praised the role of UGC as a regulator in the field of higher education but due to the congestion of work and over work-load and regulating every aspect of the higher education can be sited as the reasons why it has failed to the perform its actual role. The political interference in the matters of the UGC and even the rigidity of various governing rules of UGC like regulations related to the financial matters of the university, interference in the autonomy of higher education institutes has also led to the criticism of the Commission. The commission has been criticized on the following aspects;

- Multiplicity of roles of UGC
- MHRD's supervision in funding of universities and colleges
- Process of determination and co-ordination of academic standards
- Nature of governing rules and regulations
- Formalism and structural delays
- Barriers to the entry of new institutes
- Restrictive and destructive interference in the finances of colleges/universities
- Fee mechanism

66. Government of India(2008a), *"Report of 'The Committee to Advise on Renovation and Rejuvenation of Higher Education", Department of Higher Education, Ministry of Human Resource Development, New Delhi.*

1. **Multiplicity of Roles**: The major area of criticism of UGC and the highlighted one is of the burden of the functions UGC have. The experimentation with the role of UGC in regulation says that the multiple roles discharged by the UGC could be segregated. UGC requires un-bundling. Its funding role could be assigned to a funding council as in the case of UK. It needs to be noted that around forty-five higher education institutions have already been disbursed funds directly. UGC provides operating budget support to merely sixteen central universities, ten deemed to universities and sixty-four colleges. Experience of the last couple of years shows that many decisions on funding of central universities were taken directly by the MHRD in the central government, UGC merely disbursed funds to the central universities as per the dictates of the ministry. Under circumstances, more efficient arrangement would be for MHRD to take upon this responsibility directly and the institutional energies of the UGC could be focused elsewhere. This would also streamline reporting arrangements and reduce reporting burden on universities while maintaining the highest level of accountability for public investment.[67].

   The National Knowledge Commission Report has also criticized the UGC on the same ground as the National Knowledge Commission report quotes "India is perhaps the only country in the world where regulation in four of the five functions is carried out by one entity that is UGC. The proposed IRAHE (renamed as NCHER) shall be responsible for setting the criteria and deciding on the entry. The role of UGC will be limited disbursing public funds.[68]

---

67. Pawan Aggarwal (2006),"Higher Education in India; The Need for Change", working paper no.108,Indian Council for Research on International Economic Relations, New Delhi
68. *Government of India (2008a), op. cit.*

2. **Process of Determination and Co-ordination of Academic Standards:** UGC in its mandate pledges to maintain the academic standard of higher education in the country and this has been regarded as the main area of concern of the UGC. But due to the over burdening of function, the Commission has not been able to provide full attention to this aspect. The UGC's role of determination and coordination of academic standards could be assigned to subject level peer networks coordinated by an independent National Qualification Authority. The maintenance of academic standards could best be done through a credible accreditation system. It is seen that communities of practice would be in better position to evolve policies and develop framework to strengthen teaching, learning and research in different subject areas rather than a centralized bureaucratic agency.[69]

3. **Nature of Governing Rules and Regulations:** The review of the existing structure of regulatory system in India and the way it regulates various aspect of higher education shows that existing regulatory procedures are extremely burdensome and counter-productive[70]. The regulations are often too detailed and diminish the responsiveness of the higher education institutions to changing needs of society. The regulatory system does not take into account the new developments in higher education particularly as they relate to new providers and new form of delivery.

4. **Formalism and Structural Delays:** One of its areas of criticism is that the commission suffers from the ills like formalism and structural delays especially in the case of its funding procedures.

---

69. ibid
70. K. Sudha Rao and Mithilesh Kumar Singh, "150 years of University Education in India : Challenges Ahead", available online at http://www.aserf.org.in/presentations/150_years_of_Hr_edu.pdf

The funding system sometimes take too much time that it becomes an obstacle rather than a support. Grants in most of cases especially Five Years Plans are sanctioned in the third year of plan. It becomes very difficult for the universities and institutes to optimally spend scarce resources within two years of the Five Year Plan. One of the examples is the junior research fellowship programmes, where the beneficiaries often get their dues lately and have cumbersome procedure for seeking other grants.

UGC has been also criticized for not efficiently implementing its policies and programmes and not been able to carry its objectives within the stipulated time limit.

5. **Barriers to the Entry of New Institutes:** The barriers to the entry of new institution are really restrictive in nature. The system of authorizing entry is cumbersome. And there are extensive rules after entry, as the UGC seeks to regulate almost every aspect of an institution from fees to curriculum. The system is also based on patently irrational principles. The UGC Act section 3.1.2(a) suggests that permission for receiving grants will be accorded only if the commission is satisfied that the existing institutions in the state are not adequate to serve the need of the state[71].

6. **Restrictive and Destructive Interference in the Finances of Colleges/Universities:** The UGC's intervention and regulation in the financial matters of higher education institutes sometimes become restrictive and destructive instead of being a positive or a constructive one. It would be a good option for the institute to gain some financial support through such means as alumni contribution, licensing fees, or user charges (for facilities in universities used by people from outside). But the current UGC practice also penalizes universities for any resource mobilized

71. *Government of India (2008a), op. cit.*

with a matching deduction from the grants in aid provided to the institutions. Rather than penalizing universities for raising resources, the UGC should incentivize them. In addition, universities must have the autonomy and flexibility to mobilize resources from elsewhere by creating or using appropriate institutional mechanisms.[72]

7. **Fee Mechanism**: UGC has been very restrictive and worked on its traditional approach when it comes to the financial matter of universities. Normally a university is allowed to raise 10% of expenditure from its funding. This criticism was well described in the national knowledge commission report as it says in theory universities have the freedom to decide on the fees, in practice, however, universities have not exercised this freedom in part because of some genuine concerns about access but in larger part because of the rhetoric populism in the political process. The problem has been compounded by the UGC method of providing grants-in-aid to bridge the difference between income and expenditure. Consequently, there is no incentive for universities or colleges to raise income through higher fees as that sum would be deducted from the UGC grants.[73]

   The public universities as compared to private institutions or as compared to the recent economic position of the country charge very low fees, and ultimately become burden on public funding. The fee mechanism needs to be rationalized and up to date through price indexation, however there may be constituted some complementary mechanism for students belonging to the weaker section of the society. The commission needs to be more liberal and rational in this matter.

---

72. Government of India (2009a), "National Knowledge Commission: Report to the Nation", National Knowledge Commission, New Delhi
73. ibid

Conclusion:

The Yash Pal committee report has praised the commission as it writes in the report that only a few organizations such as the UGC took major initiatives in fostering educational innovations through its major schemes and programmes which have been responsive to the changes and challenges taking place in the higher education system. But due to the over burden of functions and multiplicity of roles it has to performs, the Commission has not been able to effectively deal with its areas of regulation. As the National Knowledge Commission report quotes "India is perhaps the only country in the world where regulation in four of the five functions is carried out by one entity that is UGC. The proposed IRAHE (renamed as NCHER) shall be responsible for setting the criteria and deciding on the entry. The role of UGC will be limited disbursing public funds.[74]

74. Government of India (2008 a),"*Report of 'The Committee to Advise on Renovation and Rejuvenation of Higher Education", department of Higher Education, Ministry of Human Resource Development, New Delhi.*

3

All India Council for Technical Education (AICTE): Emergence, Structure, functioning and its Evaluation

All India Council for Technical Education is a body providing institutional regulatory mechanism in the field of technical education and deals with all facets of technical education. This chapter deals with the emergence of AICTE, its structure and functions and concentrates on assessing the role of AICTE as a regulator in the field of technical education

Technical Education in India: Introduction

Technical education has always been significant in the course of development. This kind of education is directly connected to the promotion of professional education and vocationalization of education. The importance of the technical education has been well recognized in 'after independence era', when the country saw the inception and emergence of many colleges and universities in the field of technical education.

After independence in 1947, India embarked upon economic development. A number of technical institutions were opened in all parts of the country. During the 1980s policy shift permitted involvement of private and voluntary organizations in setting up of technical institutions on self financing basis. This ushered in as era of unprecedented growth of technical education.[75]

75. www.aicte-india.org/downloads/officeprocedure.pdf, website of AICTE

The beginning of formal Technical Education in India can be dated back to the mid 19th century. The major policy initiatives in the pre-independence period included appointment of the Indian Universities Commission in 1902, issue of the Indian Education policy resolution in 1904 and the Governor General's policy statement of 1913 stressing the importance of technical education, the establishment of Indian Institute of Science (II Sc.) in Bangalore, Institution for Sugar, Textile and Leather Technology in Kanpur, National Council of Education (N.C.E.) in Bengal in 1905 and Industrial schools in several provinces. Significant developments include:

1. Constitution of the Technical Education Committee of the Central Advisory Board of Education (CABE) of 1943;
2. Preparation of the Sergeant Report of 1944; and
3. Formation of the All India Council for Technical Education (AICTE) in 1945 by the Government of India. [76]

Technical education at all levels in the country is witnessing a consistent growth pattern marked by the setting up of new institutions and the improvement of the existing ones. This diversification and expansion of the technical education is carried forward by the introduction of The All India Council for Technical Education (AICTE). In this particular chapter we will discuss the emergence of AICTE, its structure, functioning and evaluation of its working.

All India Council for Technical Education (AICTE)

It was the need of the time to have institutional mechanism that will deal with the promotion of technical education, will provide the direction to growth of technical education in India, will response to the challenges of diversification and expansion, will provide a platform for the research and development activities in this field and will work

76. www.aicte-india.org/downloads/final_approval_process_241210.pdf, website of AICTE

for the over-all regulation in the field of technical education. The efforts in this regard paved the way for the constitution of AICTE.

The All India Council for Technical Education (AICTE), set-up in November 1945 as a national level Apex Advisory Body, marches ahead with its mission of developing and promoting quality technical education in the country in a coordinated and integrated manner. The Council is constantly endeavoring to encourage a meaningful association between the technical education system and research and development activities in a concerted effort aimed at nation-building. The Council believes in providing a proper impetus to Institutions in generating competent engineers and scientists and encourages them to think beyond the curriculum while imparting training for the advancement of knowledge[77].

AICTE, from its inception was viewed as a source which will cater to the needs of industrial development in the post independence period. Economic development and particularly, the industrial development in its course needed qualified professionals not only in the field of sciences but also such as Business Management, Architecture, Hotel Management, Pharmacy etc. This diversification was also handled by the AICTE as The Government of India decided in 1954 to set up a Board of Management Studies under AICTE to formulate standards and promote Management Education. Other major initiatives taken in Management Education include: setting up of the Administrative Staff College of India at Hyderabad in the late fifties, National Productivity Council and Indian Institution of Management in the early sixties. Architecture was covered under the Architects Act, 1972. Subsequently, for better coordination of the Professional Courses, Architecture Education was also placed under the purview of AICTE.[78]

77. *ibid*
78. *ibid*

Even earlier, the Education Commission of 1964, popularly known as Kothari Commission after the name of its Chairman, made the following recommendation for the proper administration of technical education:

"To ensure the pursuit of the highest standards at the first degree and post-graduate levels, and to provide an adequate machinery with the national and professional concern with the future development at these levels, we have recommended the setting up of a UGC-type organization, industry and concerned Ministries. This body should have a full-time chairman, and funds should be allotted to it on a block basis."[79]

The areas under the functioning of AICTE had been or have been increasing with the emergence of the needs of regulation in new emerging areas of technical education. The National Council of Hotel Management and Catering Technology were set up in 1982. The policies and programmes of AICTE underwent a continuous change in the Five Years Plan too. But till this time AICTE was an advisory body.

The Government of India (Ministry of Human Resource Development) also constituted a National Working Group to look into the role of AICTE in the context of proliferation of technical institutions, maintenance of standards and other related matters. The Working Group recommended that AICTE be vested with the necessary statutory authority for making it more effective, which would consequently require restructuring and strengthening with necessary infrastructure and operating mechanisms.[80]

It was only in 1987 that the AICTE got statutory status pursuant to the above recommendations of the National Working Group, as the All India Council for Technical Education Act, 1987 was

79. http://www.aicte-india.org/aboutaicte.htm, Website of AICTE
80. ibid

enacted to provide for the establishment of an All India Council for Technical Education with a view to the proper planning and co-ordinate development of technical education system throughout the country, the promotion of qualitative improvement of such education in relation to planned quantitative growth and regulation and proper maintenance of norms and standards in the technical education system and for matter connected herewith. The Act came into force w.e.f. March 28. 1988. The statutory All India Council for Technical Education was established on May 12, 1988.[81]

AICTE's Vision

Be a world class organization leading technological and socioeconomic development of the Country by enhancing the global competitiveness of technical manpower, by ensuring high quality technical education to all sections of the society[82].

Mission of AICTE

1. Transparent governance and accountability in approach towards society.
2. Planned and coordinated development of Technical Education in the Country by ensuring world-class standards of Institutions through accreditation.
3. Facilitating world-class Technical Education through:
    i. Development of high quality Institutions, academic excellence and innovative research and development programs;
    ii. Networking of Institutions for optimum resource utilization;

81. www.aicte-india.org/downloads/final_approval_process_241210.pdf, *op.cit.*
82. *Ibid*

iii. Dissemination of knowledge;

iv. Technology forecasting and global manpower planning;

v. Promotion of industry-Institution interaction for developing new products, services, and patents;

vi. Inculcating entrepreneurship;

vii. Encouraging indigenous technology;

viii. Focusing on non-formal education;

ix. Providing affordable education to all.

x. Making Indian Technical Education globally acceptable.

xi. A vision of a forward-looking organization that has an efficient, flexible and empowered manpower, sensitive to stakeholder's expectations.[83]

Objectives of AICTE

The main objectives of All India Council for Technical Education are stated below:

1. Promotion of Quality in Technical Education
2. Planned and coordinated development of technical education system in the country
3. Regulation and maintenance of norms and standards in technical education system

Composition of AICTE

The AICTE as an organization gives representation to every area, every Board, Council and every other organization related to or working in the field of technical education. The Council has also involved the chairman of some other important organizations, working in the field of education in order to have their guidance support in its endeavors.

---

83. *ibid*

This is the reason that it has long list of members and ex-officio members. The AICTE Act provides for the detailed composition of the Council. The members will include:

1. A Chairman to be appointed by the Central Government
2. A Vice-Chairman to be appointed by the Central Government

   The ex-officio members include;

3. The Secretary of the Government of India in the ministry of the central government with education
4. The Education Advisor (General) to the Govt. of India
5. The Chairman of four Regional committees
6. The Chairman of the following Boards;
   i. The All India Board of Vocational Education
   ii. The All India Board of Technical Education
   iii. The All India Board of Under graduate studies in Engineering and Technology
   iv. The All India Board of Post Graduate Education and Research in Engineering and Technology
   v. The All India Board of Management and studies
7. The Chairman, University Grants Commission
8. The Director, Institute of Applied Manpower Research
9. The Director-General, Indian Council of Agricultural Research
10. The Director-General, Council of Scientific and Industrial Research

    Other members of the AICTE include:

11. One member to be appointed by the Central Government to represent the Ministry of Finance of the Central Government
12. One member to be appointed by the Central Government to represent the Ministry of Science and Technology of the Central Govt.

13. Four members to be appointed by the Central Government by rotation to represent the Ministries and Departments of the Central Government, other than those specified in clause 11 and 12
14. Two members of Parliament of whom one is to be elected by the house of the people and one by the council of the states.
15. Eight members to be appointed by the Central Government by rotation in alphabetical order to represent the states and UTs. Appointment under this is to be made on the recommendation of the states and UTs concerned.
16. Four members to be appointed by the Central Government to represent the organization in the field of Industry and Commerce.
17. Seven member to be appointed by the Central Government to represent the following;
    i. The Central Advisory Board of Education
    ii. The Association of Indian Universities.
    iii. The Indian Society for Technical Education
    iv. The Council of Indian Institutes of Technology
    v. The Pharmacy Council of India
    vi. The National Productivity council
    vii. The Council of Architecture
18. Four member to be appointed by the Central Government to represent the professional bodies in the field of Technical Education
19. Not more than two members to be appointed by the Central Government to represent such interests not covered by the foregoing clauses as the Central Government may deem fit.
20. Member-secretary to be appointed by the Central Government

The Act provides the term of three years for the members of the council, except for the ex-officio members. In the absence of chairman, vice-chairman will perform his functions. The council will meet at such times and places and will observe such rules of procedure in regards to the transaction of business at its meeting as may be provided by the regulation.[84]

Organization of AICTE

The AICTE came into existence as a national level apex body to stimulate, coordinate and control the provision of facilities for technical education needed for industrial development in the post-war period in the country. Then with the introduction of National Policy on Education (1986) increased its scope of activities as it stipulated that AICTE be vested with statutory authority for planning, formulation and maintenance of norms and standards assurance through accreditation, funding in priority areas, monitoring and evaluation, maintaining parity of certification and awards and ensuring coordinated and integrated development and management of technical education in the country. With the passage of time other boards and councils also roped in under the AICTE. The council in order to be responsive to all its duties has structured itself with the executive committee, boards, regional committees and national board for accreditation. The brief introduction to these bodies is given below:

1. **Executive committee:** The Executive Committee is a 21 member body constituted by the Council and discharges such function as assigned by the Council from time to time. The Executive Committee is chaired by the Chairman of the Council and Vice Chairman of the Council takes the same place in the Council. The Member Secretary of the AICTE is also the Member Secretary of the Executive Committee.

84. www.aicte-india.org.in, website of AICTE

2. **Boards of Studies:** The AICTE provides for the establishment of five Boards of Studies. In addition five more Boards were established for other disciplines of technical education. The Boards advise the Executive Committee on academic matters falling in their areas of concern including norms, standards, model curricula, model facilities, structure of course etc. the council has established following Boards of Studies;

   i. All India Board of Vocational Education
   ii. All India Board of Technical Education
   iii. All India Board of Under-Graduate Studies in Engineering and Technology
   iv. All India Board of Post-Graduate Studies in Engineering and Technology
   v. All India Board Of Management Studies Initially, the AICTE Act provided for the establishment of five Boards of Studies. Later, four more Boards of Studies were added by the Council and subsequently one more Board has been added.
   vi All India Board Hotel Management and Catering Technology
   vii. All India Board Information Technology Education
   viii. All India Board Pharmaceutical Education
   ix. All India Board Town and Country Planning
   x. All India Board Architecture

3. **Regional Committees:** The Council has 8 Regional Committees by now concerning different geographical regions. The Regional Committees assist and advise the Council in all aspects of planning, promoting and regulating technical education within their respective regions. Each Regional Committee is a 15-20

member body headed by a person of eminence. The Council has the following Regional Committees;

i. The Northern Regional Committee with its office at Kanpur,

ii. The Southern Regional Committee with its office at Madras,

iii. The Western Regional Committee with its office at Bombay

iv. The Eastern Regional Committee with its office at Kolkata

v. Central Regional Committee with its office at Bhopal

vi. North Western Regional Committee with its office at Chandigarh

vii. South Central Regional Committee with its office at Andhra Pradesh

viii. South Western Regional Committee with its office at Bangalore

4. **National Board of Accreditation:** The Council has set up through a resolution of Councils/Executive Committees periodically conduct evaluation of technical institution or programmes on the basis of guidelines, norms and standards specified by it for quality assessment.

The functions of the National Board of Accreditation are:

i. To make recommendations with regard to issues of quality assurance and quality management in technical education in India.

ii. To prescribe guidelines, norms and standards for the purpose of accreditation of technical education programmes / institutions.

iii. To advise the Executive Committee/Council regarding de-recognition of an institution or a programme based on the evaluation conducted as per the prescribed procedure for the purpose.

iv. To advise and assist the Executive Committee/Council on policies and parameters pertaining to the accreditation process.

v. To advise the Executive Committee/Council on formulation of schemes for Promotion of Qualitative Improvements in Technical Education.

vi. To carry out any other function assigned by the Executive Committee/ Council.

The National Board of Accreditation shall make suitable recommendations in the discharge of the above functions to the Executive committee / Council in accordance with the procedure prescribed from time to time.

5. **Bureaus:** The AICTE comprises of eight Bureaus, namely;

i. Engineering & Technology (E&T) Bureau,

ii. Management & Technology (M&T) Bureau,

iii. Quality Assurance (QA) Bureau,

iv. Planning and Coordination(PC) Bureau,

v. Research and Institutional Development (RID) Bureau,

vi. Academic (Acad.)Bureau,

vii. Administration (Admin) Bureau and

viii. Finance (Fin) Bureau. Each Bureau.

Each bureau is headed by an Adviser/Director, who is assisted by technical and other staff. The multidiscipline technical staff is taken either on deputation or on contract from various Government Departments, University Grants Commission, academic institutions etc. Computers are appropriately provided to each bureau for work. These computers are networked through LAN for retrieval and exchange of information. Cleaning and maintenance, security, transport, hospitality and canteen services are provided by external agencies. [85]

The council, the executive committee, All India Boards of Studies and Regional Committees are all of the statutory nature. All these bodies have well defined rationale behind their inception or emergence. These bodies provided the AICTE with much needed structural changes and brought the decentralization in the working of AICTE. All its bodies have their specific tasks and provide the council assistance in planning, promoting and regulating technical education.

Responsibilities of AICTE

The responsibilities entrusted to the AICTE, defined in the AICTE Act are.

1. Give proper directions for proper planning and coordinated development of the technical education system in the country.
2. Promotion of qualitative improvements in relation to planned quantitative growth of technical education.
3. Review, regulation and maintenance of norms and standards in the technical education system and matters connected therewith.
4. Assessment of manpower requirement.
5. To liaise with state governments, universities and other statutory bodies.
6. Others as provided in the Act.[86]

85. ibid
86. www.aicte-india.org/downloads/final_approval_process_241210.pdf, *op.cit*

Functions of AICTE

As stated above that the functions of the AICTE increased over the period of the time or since its inception it has been involving all the facets of technical education in India. The challenges of the expansions and then the emergence of new areas in the field of technical education led to increase in the functions of AICTE. Even the policies and programmes related to the development of technical education have been changing in the Five-Year Plans. Education in other professional fields such as, Pharmacy, Applied Arts & Crafts has also undergone similar developments during the post-independence period. Programs for Technical Education, during the first three Five Year Plans, were devoted to expansion of technical education to meet the growing demand for technical personnel at Diploma, Degree and Post-Graduate Levels. From the fourth Five Year Plan onwards, the emphasis was shifted to the improvement of quality and standard of technical education. This was done through implementation of the Quality Improvement Program consisting of three major components that provided for M.E. / M. Tech and Ph. D Programs, Establishment of Curriculum Design and Development Cells, and Short Term Training Programs.

The Council has been entrusted with all such functions and is required take all such steps which the Council considers are necessary for ensuring coordinated and integrated development of technical and management education and maintenance of standards. To achieve this target, the commission performs functions accordingly. The detailed analysis of the functions of AICTE as devised in the AICTE Act is as following:

1. To undertake surveys in various fields of technical education, collect data on all matters and make forecast of the needed growth and development of technical education in the country at all levels.

2. To coordinate the development of technical education at all levels
3. To allocate and disburse out the funds and grants of the council on such terms it considers fit to the following institutions
   i. Technical institutions
   ii. Universities imparting technical education in coordination with the council.
4. To promote innovation, research and development in established and new technologies, generations, adaption and adaption of new technologies to meet developmental requirements and for over-all improvement of educational process.
5. To formulate schemes for promoting technical education for women, handicapped and weaker sections of the society.
6. To promote an effective link between technical education systems and other relevant systems including research and development organizations, industry and the community.
7. To evolve suitable performance appraisal systems for technical institution and universities imparting technical education incorporating norms and mechanism for enforcing accountability.
8. To formulate schemes for the initials and in service training of teachers and identify institutions or centers and set up new centers for offering staff development programmes including continuing education of teachers.
9. To lay down norms and standards for course, curricula, physical and instructional facilities, staff pattern, staff qualifications, quality instructions, assessment and examinations.
10. To fix norms and guidelines for charging tuition and other fees
11. To grant approval for starting new technical institutions and

for introduction of new courses or programmes in consultation with the agencies concerned.

12. Advise the central Government in respect of grants of charter to any professional body or institution in the field of technical education conferring powers, rights and privileges on it for the promotion of such professions in its field including conduct of examinations and awarding of membership certificates.
13. To lay down norms for granting autonomy to technical education.
14. To take all necessary steps to prevent commercialization of technical education.
15. To provide guidelines for admission of students to technical institutions and universities imparting technical education.
16. To inspect or cause to inspect any technical institutions and universities imparting technical education.
17. To withhold or discontinue grants in respect of courses, programmes to such technical institutions which fails to comply with the direction given by the council within the stipulated period of time and take such other steps as may be necessary for ensuring compliance of the directions of the council
18. To take steps to strengthen the existing organization and to set up new organizations, to ensure effective discharge of the council's responsibilities and to create positions of professional, technical and supporting staff based on requirements.
19. To declare technical institutions fit at various levels and types offering courses in technical education to receive grants.
20. To advise the commission for declaring any institutions imparting technical education as a deemed university.
21. To set up a National Board of Accreditation to periodically conduct evaluation of technical institutions or programmes

on the basis of guidelines, norms and standards specified by it and to make recommendation to it or the council, or to the commission or to other bodies, regarding recognition or de-recognition of the institutions or the programmes.

22. For the purpose of ascertaining needs of technical institution or a university or its standards of teaching, examination and research, the council may cause an inspection of any departments of such technical institution or university to be made in such manner as may be prescribed and by such person or persons as it may direct.
23. The council has been entrusted with the task of preparing its annual budget showing the estimated receipts and expenditure.
24. The council prepares its annual report every year giving a true and full account of its activities during the previous years.
25. It is the responsibility of the council to maintain its accounts in consultation with Comptroller and Auditor General of India, and the audit of the accounts is done by the same authority.
26. To perform such other functions as may be prescribed.

The purview of AICTE covers programmes of technical education including training and research in Engineering & Technology, Architecture & Town Planning, Management, Pharmacy, Applied Arts and Crafts, Hotel Management and Catering Technology etc. at different levels.[87]

Assessment of the AICTE's Role as a Regulator in Higher Education:

The council deals with all those areas of higher education which comes under the technical education arena. The emergence of AICTE has been viewed as a institution which will deal with all the areas of

87. http://www.aicte-india.org.in, op.cit.

technical educations, will oversee its expansion and growth, will provide sufficient infrastructural arrangement, will look forward to the diversification and advancements in technical educations and will be responsible for the promotion of technical education, last but not the least will work as a overall regulator in the field of technical education. In its way towards regulating the technical education, the AICTE has got praise on various accounts also criticized on some grounds.

The main areas of focus of AICTE in regulation are or on which we will focus in this particular chapter are;

1. Providing approval to the new entrants, checking out their credentials,
2. Maintenance of academic standards, punishing those involved in malpractices
3. To coordinate with the states on matters related to technical education
4. Promoting innovations and research and development
5. Engaging technical education with industry and research community
6. Regulation of schemes for the faculty development
7. Conducting relevant studies
8. Regulating the foreign institutes in the area of technical education
9. Regulating the fee structure

Here we will briefly discuss the above mentioned areas of regulation of AICTE;

1. **Providing Approval to the New Entrants, Checking out their Credentials:** In accordance with the functions assigned to it under Clause 10(k) of the AICTE Act, the Council grants approvals for starting new technical institutions and for introducing new courses or programmes in already approved

institutions. Approvals are accorded in consultation with respective State Governments and affiliating universities. The AICTE has been so far very active and alert when it comes to provide approval to the new institutions of technical education. Approval process is facilitated by the inspection and the institutes which lack the specified criteria are rejected by the Council. In the recent venture of its approval process, in April 2012, in order to expedite the admission process for professional courses, the council approved 102 new colleges of technical education. The move claimed to create over 2.5 lakh new seats for the professionals. AICTE chairman SS Mantha claimed to have received 699 proposals for approval including those of architecture, management and pharmacy. Thus the council from time to time reviews the need of strengthening the infrastructural arrangement in its way towards promoting the technical education in the country.[88]

2. **Maintenance of Academic Standards, Punishing those Involved in Malpractices:** The council has the responsibility of maintaining the standards of technical education in the country. And this includes the maintenance of the academic standards and ethical and moral standards. The council has been responsive to the case of those institutions involved in ill practices and has rejected their approval. In one of its recent move, in April 2012, in a bid to crack down on corruption in technical education institutes, the All India Council for Technical Education (AICTE) has cancelled recognition of five engineering colleges affiliated to Rajasthan Technical University (RTU) on grounds of their involvement in malpractices. The colleges' include-Bansal Engineering College in Jaipur, Lords Management College, Lords Engineering College and Lords

88. Times of India (2012a), "All India Council for Technical Education gives nod to 102 college" 18th April, New Delhi

Hospitality College in Alwar and one engineering college run by Chachan Educational Society. These colleges were running without approval since 2010-11. The AICTE had cancelled affiliations granted after CBI filed cases against these institutes in different cases from cheating to bribery. According to the new policy introduced in February last year (2011), AICTE prevents continuation of affiliation to colleges that were booked by a Central investigation agency on corruption charges. Most of the students studying here are from rural background and the surrounding areas.[89]

3. **Inspection of Institutes:** Providing approval to the institutes of technical education is not the end in itself, AICTE regulates the standards of the institutions, and carries inspection from time to time. In its recent initiatives the council started carrying inspection of those institutions which were seeking increase in the seats of various courses of management and engineering. Conventionally, the colleges apply for hike in intake of seats on the web portal of AICTE furnishing details of the infrastructure, staff and students online. The applications are scrutinized online and permission given for additional seats. However, following complaints that many colleges do not have infrastructure and human resource that match the details provided in the online application, the AICTE decided to carry out surprise raids. In the past three years, many colleges are reported to have indulged in malpractices including lying about infrastructure and human resource. AICTE warned that colleges which are found flouting norms or providing incorrect information will be penalized. [90]

---

89. Times of India (2012b), "AICTE cancels nod to 5 engineering colleges" 21st April, 2012, New Delhi
90. Times of India (2012c), "AICTE raids colleges to verify online claims", 11th April, 2012, New Delhi

4. **To Coordinate with the States on Matters Related to Technical Education**: In its approval procedure it also entertains the demands of the respective states. In March 2012, Several State Governments had requested AICTE not to clear the applications for starting new engineering colleges. They have cited the incidence of growing number of vacant BE/BTech seats in the existing colleges. Tamil Nadu, Andhra Pradesh and Odisha are among the States which are opposed to opening of new technical institutions as there has been an exponential growth in the number of colleges, while the demand for admission has scaled down in recent years. Besides, managing quality in the existing institutions has become a tough task for the regulatory authorities. So the council has taken a decision not to sanction approval for new applicants from 2013-14 for these states.[91]

5. **Promoting Innovations in Research and Development**: The research and development aspect of technical education and its promotion has been given the deserved importance in AICTE's programmes over the years. Through Clauses 10 (c) and 10(d) of the AICTE Act, the Council promotes innovations and research and development in established and new technologies; generation, adoption and adaptation of new technologies to meet developmental requirements of the country and for the overall improvement of educational process. Towards these ends, the Council operates three schemes, namely, Modernization and Removal of Obsolescence (MODROBS), Research Promotion Scheme (RPS) and Nationally Coordinated Projects (NCP). A total of 544 Projects were approved for financial support under MODROBS and RPS schemes during the year 2008-2009 and the Council released a total amount of Rs.3594.07 Lakh.

91. Times of India (2012d), "AICTE may bar new engineering, management colleges from 2014", 14th March, New Delhi

The projects sanctioned under the above research schemes are reviewed each year in monitoring meetings to ensure effective implementation of projects and proper utilization of grants.[92]

The Council from time to time engages itself with other institutes of excellence in order to promote the quality research in technical education. In one of its recent initiative, Adding value to government's skill development initiative, the AICTE roped in Tata Institute of Social Sciences (TISS) to conduct studies on skill requirements and develop content for various sectors. TISS will not only conduct research into vocational education but will develop teaching methodologies and pedagogy, work in the area of training the trainers and develop methodology for skill assessment and skill accreditation. A MoU was signed in this regard between the All India Council for Technical Education (AICTE) and TISS in the presence of HRD Minister Kapil Sibal.[93]

In it's another endeavor, and in an effort to provide students, faculty and educational institutions with free access to development software, the All India Council for Technical Education in October, 2010 signed an agreement with two private players to improve learning in the field. With the signing of the agreement, AICTE, Autodesk and Microsoft have become partner to deliver free access to development software and design software for institutions, students and faculty in the country.[94]

---

92. All India Council for Technical Education (2008-09 a.), Annual Report 2008-09, New Delhi, p.
93. The Economic Times(2012a), "AICTE signs MoU with TISS on skill development", 27th March, New Delhi
94. The Economic Times (2008b), "AICTE to come out with guidelines on uniform fee structure", New Delhi

6. **Engaging Technical Education with Industry and Research Community**: The Council promotes effective link between technical education system and other relevant systems, including industry and research community. For the purpose, the Council operates various schemes; Industry Institute Partnership Cell (IIPC), Entrepreneurship Development Cell (EDC), and National Facilities in Engineering and Technology with Industrial Collaboration (NAFETIC). Its recent collaboration with Microsoft has already made the news. The All India Council for Technical Education (AICTE) and Microsoft Corporation announced that the AICTE will deploy Microsoft Live@edu, a cloud-based solution over the next three months to more than 10,000 technical colleges and institutes throughout India. The cloud deployment will expand students' access to high-quality technical education and collaboration. Microsoft's cloud platform will make for a truly progressive ecosystem and contribute to the country's technical education by providing a better communication and collaboration platform for institutes and students.[95]
7. **Regulation of Schemes for the Faculty Development**: There are several schemes for faculty development, namely, Quality Improvement Programme (QIP), Career Award for Young Teachers (CAYT), Emeritus Fellowship, Visiting Professorship, Seminar Grant, Travel Grant, Staff Development Programme, National Doctoral Fellowship, AICTE-INAE Distinguished Visiting Professorship and Financial Assistance to Professional Societies/ Bodies. Under the Quality Improvement Programme (QIP), faculty members of degree level institutions are given opportunity to upgrade their qualifications to Master's and Ph.D.

95. Times of India (2012e), "AICTE adopts cloud-based solution", 13th April, New Delhi

levels. Under the Scheme QIP (poly), polytechnic teachers can pursue Master's degree programmes. Courseware Development and other short term training programmes are also conducted under the QIP Scheme. In the Emeritus Fellowship scheme, superannuated faculty members are supported for two years to continue research through grant of fellowships and contingency grants. Under the scheme of Visiting Professorship, reputed academicians and technologists provide required expertise to their host institutions. Financial assistance is provided to regular faculty through schemes of Career Award for Young Teachers, Travel Grant and Seminar Grant. The Staff Development Programmes help new teachers to further enhance teaching skills. Professional Societies/Bodies are also provided non-recurring grants for various purposes. The scheme of AICTE-INAE Distinguished Visiting Professorship jointly initiated by the AICTE and the Indian National Academy of Engineering (INAE) helps institutions avail expertise from experienced professionals from industry.[96]

8. **Conducting Relevant Studies**: The availability of reliable data of the various field of technical education has also been important in policy process and has been one of the main concerns of AICTE. National Technical Manpower Information System (NTMIS) operates with a view to generate and maintain reliable data and information needed for prospective planning of technical education on the basis of demand and supply positions. The objectives assigned to NTMIS include estimation of short term and long-term demands of various categories of engineering and technical manpower, their supply, identification of anticipated gaps in demand and supply, and assessment of the adequacy of

96. All India Council for Technical Education (2008-09 a.), Annual Report 2008-09, op. cit., pp.17

the current enrolment rate in respect of each of the engineering and technical manpower categories.[97]

9. **Regulating the Foreign Institutes in the Area of Technical Education:** The Council made regulations for regulating entry and operation of Foreign Universities/ Institutions imparting technical education in India. This Regulation known as 'AICTE Regulations for Entry and Operation of Foreign Universities in India imparting technical education, 2005' were formulated primarily to check and avoid illegal entry of unscrupulous persons using/misusing the name of Foreign University/ Institution for unlawful gains. To safeguard the interest of all stakeholders, a public notice was issued in all leading newspapers on 5th May, 2005 directing the foreign universities operating in India to comply with the above regulations. Communications were sent to all India institutions collaborating with foreign universities/ institutions based on media advertisement, directing them to comply with regulations 2005.[98]

10. **Regulating the Fee Structure:** In 2008 the council initiated the process of setting guidelines on uniform fee structure for technical education across the country, responding to appeals made by the Consortium of Self-Financed Professional, Arts and Sciences Colleges in Tamil Nadu.[99]

Critical Evaluation

The areas on which AICTE has been criticized are as followed;

1. Involvement of unfair practices in approval practice

---

97. All India Council for Technical Education (2008-09 a.), Annual Report 2008-09, op. cit., pp.19
98. Ibid., pp.20
99. The Economic Times (2008b), "AICTE to come out with guidelines on uniform fee structure", New Delhi

2. Employability issues; Council's inefficiency
3. Failure in maintaining the standards of technical education

1. **Involvement of Unfair Practices in Approval Process:** The AICTE has been the centre of criticism over the period of time for some of its activities. In 2008, as the watchdog for technical education, AICTE has been deeply criticized for its 'unfair' practices in the past. While AICTE is known to have approved institutions with dubious antecedents, it has not recognized some of India's premier institutes like Indian School of Business (ISB), Hyderabad, and SP Jain, Mumbai.[100]
2. **Employability Issues; Council's Inefficiency**: Another criticism came from the Parliamentary Committee in the same year as the Council was termed as inefficient because of the employability issues. The Committee has voiced concern over "employability" of students passing out of technical institutions in the country, saying the expected response from the industry is "simply missing". Despite several initiatives taken for meaningful interaction between industry and academia for mutual benefits specific to technical education system, linkages between industry and technical institutions continue to remain weak, the Committee said. It was said that the council was mainly responsible for this failure.[101]
3. **Failure in Maintaining the Standards of Technical Education:** The Council has been unresponsive or failed to stop and check the mushrooming of ill standards institutes in the field of technical education. It has happened many times that the institutes which were approved by the AICTE later it came to

---

100. The Economic Times (2008c), "AICTE comes under Government scrutiny", 31st January, New Delhi
101. The Economic Times (2008d), "Concern over employability of tech students: Panel", 14th December, New Delhi

light that the institutes lacked on many ground. According to a report of the Comptroller and Auditor General of India, each of the 171 new institutions that were audited failed on one or more pre-requisites of the AICTE. Over the last 5 years, the AICTE has approved 1,829 new institutions, of these only 171 were audited. The deficiencies found by the audit team range from inadequate classroom size, absence of basic facilities, library and laboratory equipment, and often the faculty was yet to be identified and hired. In 10 instances, the institute had no principal. The most common problem was the absence of faculty, while nearly 50% of the audited institutes had no proper library facilities. In most cases, the deficiencies were pointed out by the expert committees constituted by AICTE. However, in a number of cases, the council approved the institution despite its own expert committee rejecting the proposal. The Electronics Research and Development Centre of India, Noida, and 3 institutes in Tamil Nadu — National Power Training Institute, Nayveli; Bharathi Dasan Engineering College, Vellore; Lakshmi Chand Rajani College of Engineering and Technology, Thiruvallur were all rejected at the proposal stage because of inadequate infrastructure and facilities. The CAG report charges the AICTE with subverting its own procedures.[102]

Conclusion:

The All India Council for Technical Education regulates all the facets of technical education; promoting innovation, accelerating research and development in the field of technical education, maintaining the standards of technical education and engaging technical education with industry and research community. However the Council has been criticized as it was known to be indulged in unfair practices

102. The Economic Times (2003e), "New engineering colleges fail to meet AICTE norms," 25th May, New Delhi

and in some cases it has been learnt and observed that the Council compromised in the maintenance of described standards as some ill standards institutes were also provided approval. The council needs to take care of all these happenings taking place which has somehow spoiled the image of AICTE.

4

Medical Council of India: As a Regulator; Introduction, organization, functioning and its assessment

Introduction

Medical education has been one of the prominent fields of higher education system. The expansion of medical education has been widely noticed. In order to regulate medical education in India, Medical Council of India was formed in 1934 under the Indian Medical Council Act, 1933. This chapter analyses the inception and evolution of MCI, its structure and functions. The chapter also evaluates the role of Medical Council as a regulator in the field of medical education.

Medical Education: Introduction

Medical education is an important aspect of education system. It has been given significant importance worldwide. In most of the countries medical education began with the informal system of education, and every country worked toward formalizing medical education by providing it institutional set up. The regulation of medical education was the next step in the area of medical education. The emerging need of medical education or promotion of medical education may be the reason, medical education became one of the famous disciplines and the time has seen wide expansion in this field. Every education system seeks to have a regulatory mechanism which will oversee the functions namely, maintenance of academic standards in that field, will form rules and regulation for the entry of new firms (institutes), will do the monitoring of these institutions and will perform the task of evaluation of their performance, will work to define mode of funding to these institutions, will regulate on their financial matters too, and more importantly will promote the research and development in this specific areas. These were also the reasons behind the realization on the part of India to have regulatory body in the field of medical education.

Inception and Evolution of Medical Council of India

It was in the British rule that The Medical Council of India was established in 1934 under the Indian Medical Council Act, 1933, now repealed, with the main function of establishing uniform standards of higher qualifications in medicine and recognition of medical qualifications in India and abroad. This development however was the first step and was in accordance to the need of that particular time. But over the period of time the country's medical education system was affected with the diversification in the field of medical education and consequent expansion.

The number of medical colleges had increased steadily during the years after Independence. It was felt that the provisions of Indian Medical Council Act were not adequate to meet with the challenges posed by the very fast development and the progress of medical education in the country. As a result, in 1956, the old Act was repealed and a new one was enacted. Some amendments to this Act were made in 1958 (36 of 1958) and in 1964 (24 of 1964). Amendments were made through an ordinance promulgated by the President of India on 27th August 1992. Through this ordinance, new section i.e. Section 10A, 10B, & Section 10C were introduced in the I.M.C. Act, 1956 notified on 2nd January 1993 mainly to restrict the mushrooming of medical colleges, increase of seats in courses and starting of new courses without the prior approval of the Government of India, Ministry of Health & Family Welfare. This amendment was duly notified by the

Government of India in the extraordinary Gazette of India part II section I on 3rd April 1993 with effective date 1st June 1992.

An amendment was made and notified by the Central Govt. duly published in the Gazette of India on 28.6.2003 regarding the Screening Test Regulations, 2002 stating that a candidate shall have to pass all the three papers in the same attempt. However, there shall not be any restriction on the number of attempts to appear in the test.

Another amendment was made and notified by the Central Govt. duly published in Gazette of India on 1st March, 2004 with regard to amend the Regulations on Graduate Medical Education, 1997 stating that there shall be no admission of students in respect of any academic session beyond 30th September under any circumstances. The Universities shall not register any student admitted beyond the said date. The Medical Council of India may direct, that any students identified as having obtained admission after the last date of closure of admission be discharged from the course of study, or any medical qualification granted to such a student shall not be a recognized qualification for the purpose of the Indian Medical Council Act, 1956. The Institution which grants admission to any student after the last date specified from the same shall also be liable to face such action as may be prescribed by MCI including surrender of seats equivalent to the extent of such admission made from its sanctioned intake capacity for the succeeding academic year". Amendment was made and Notified by the Central Govt. duly published in the Gazette of India on 23rd March, 2006 with regard to Postgraduate Medical Education (Amendment) Regulations, 2006.

Latest Amendment were made and notified by the Central Govt. duly published in the Gazette of India on 8.7.2009, 21.7.2009, 21.7.2009, 3.8.2009, 26.8.2009, 23,9,2009, 23.9.2009, 25.9.2009, 6.10.2009, 22.10.2009, 28.10.2009. 28.10.2009, 13.11.2009, 17.11.2009, 9.12.2009, 9.12.2009, 10.12.2009, 15.12.2009, 29.12.2009, 11.1.2010, 18.1.2010, 30.1.2010, 30.1.2010, 30.1.2010,

26.2.2010, 26.2.2010, 26.2.2010 and 26.2.2010. In India there are 205 recognized medical colleges, and 65 colleges have been permitted u/s 10A of the Indian Medical Council Act, 1956 during the year under review. Approximately 28158 graduates pass out every year from these colleges. Such graduates after completing compulsory rotating internship are required to be registered with State Medical Council or the Medical Council of India to practice medicine in the country.[103]

Objectives of the Council

The Council came into existence as a main body regulating the standards of institutions of medical education and maintenance of the devised standards through the various mediums of regulations of the council. The main objectives of the Council are:

1. Maintenance of uniform standards of medical education, both undergraduate and postgraduate. It also envisages inspections/visitations of medical colleges for permission to start medical colleges for MBBS course, starting of new Postgraduate courses and increase of seats (as per provisions of section 10A of the Act).
2. Recommendation for recognition/de-recognition of medical qualifications of medical institutions (a) within, (b) outside the country After amendment of section 13(4) which provides for screening test, scope of recognition of foreign medical qualifications when held by Indian nationals has basic more or less met a dead end. In the matter of mutual recognition of Medical qualifications as per provisions of section 12 (2) of the Act, matters can still be considered.
3. Permanent registration/provisional registration of doctors with recognized medical qualifications,

103. Medical Council of India (2009-10 a.), Annual Report, 2009-10, New Delhi, pp.1

4. Reciprocity with foreign countries in the matter of mutual recognition of medical qualifications.
5. Maintenance of Indian Medical Register.
6. Issue of good standing certificates.[104]

Composition of the Council

The MCI Act 1956 describes the composition of the Council. Section 3(1) of the Indian Medical Council Act, 1956 provides for constitution and composition of the Council consisting of the following:-

(a) One member from each State other than a Union Territory to be nominated by the Central Government in consultation with the State Government concerned.

(b) One member from each University, to be elected from amongst the members of the medical faculty of the University or in case the University has no Senate, by members of the Court.

(c) One member; from each State- in which a State Medical Register is maintained-to be elected from amongst themselves by persons enrolled on such Register – who possess the medical qualifications included in the First and Second Schedule or in Part-II of the third Schedule to the Act.

(d) Seven members to be elected from amongst themselves by persons who possess the medical qualification included in the Part I of the Third Schedule.

(e) Eight members to be nominated by the Central Government.[105]

Out of the total number of 148 membership of the Council, names of 19 universities have been deleted vide Central Govt. Notifications dated 27.3.2000, 17.5.2000, 25.7.2000 & 19.7.2001.

104. Ibid., pp.2

105. www.mciindia.org/ActsandAmendments/The Medical Council Act 1956.aspx, website of MCI

Hence, total number of membership is 129, out of which 35 seats are lying vacant due to various reasons like expiry of term, non-election of a member, nonexistence of medical faculty of certain Universities due to establishment of concerned State Health and Universities. [106]

Organization of the Council

The Council works through two main Committees; Executive Committee and the Postgraduate Medical Education Committee. The later has five divisions under it which deal with the various aspects; migration, describing teaching eligibility qualifications, finance, ethics etc. the brief discussion on these committees is as following:

1. **Executive Committee:** Composition of the Executive Committee is – 4 members amongst University representatives, 3 members from amongst nominated members, 2 members from amongst representative of Registered Medical Graduate and one member of the Licentiate Group. The President and the Vice-President of the Council are ex-officio members of the Executive Committee.
2. **The Postgraduate Medical Education Committee:** Composition of the Postgraduate Committee is – 6 members are nominated by the Central Govt. and three members are elected by the Council from amongst its members. The main issues taken up by this committee are
   i. Starting off & increase in intake capacity in various Postgraduate courses and
   ii. Recognition of Postgraduate qualifications, considering matters of continuation of recognition of Postgraduate qualification of various subjects

---

106. Medical Council of India (2009-10 a.), Annual Report, 2009-10, op. cit., 5

iii. Prescribing broad framework of syllabus and details of curriculum and fixing appropriate clinical material for various Postgraduate degree/diploma courses

iv. Making appropriate recommendations to the Central Government with due approval by the General Body of the Council.

Frequency of Meeting of Executive Committee and of Postgraduate Committee on an average has now increased to once every month. In addition to the above mentioned two important and statutory Committees of the Council, there are certain Sub-committees to facilitate smooth functioning of the connected activities within the frame work of various Regulations and Policy decisions of the Council. The details of such Sub-committees are as under:-

a. **Migration Sub-Committee:** Though migration as a matter of principle are not encouraged by the Council, yet under the Regulations of the Council on Graduate Medical Education, 1997 there is a provision for migration of students at Undergraduate level from one recognized medical college to another recognized medical college with certain other conditions. The Migration Sub-Committee of the Council is entrusted with the job of consideration of genuine and legitimate migrations of the Candidates; whose applications are received by the office and dealt with as per provisions of 6 the Council Regulations. The office received 15 applications and allowed migration of 6 students only.

b. **Teacher's Eligibility Qualification Sub-Committee:** Council has prescribed minimum qualifications and teaching experience for recruitment of teachers in a medical college and further promotions in the teaching cadre. The matters, which cannot be decided by the appointing authorities (i.e. Universities or colleges etc.), are referred to this Sub-Committee for consideration.

c. **Finance Sub-Committee:** This is another important Sub-committee of the Council which decides upon the matters pertaining to finance of the Council in terms of preparation of budget, expenditure, implementation of Central Government orders with respect to service conditions etc.

d. **Ethics Sub-Committee:** The present day scenario has changed and as a result of the Consumer Protection Act, 1988 made applicable to the practicing physicians, complaints against doctors have increased manifold. The Council received 769 matters of ethical nature during the year under review. Out of 769 complaints, 254 have been referred to the concerned State Councils/Authorities for necessary action, 21 of these are awaiting clarification/details from complainants and/ or comments from the concerned Doctors etc. while 494 complaints stand disposed by this Council.

e. **Continuing Medical Education Advisory Committee:** In 1985 a Continuing Medical Education Cell was set up in the Medical Council of India – duly approved by the Central Government, Ministry of Health & Family Welfare, New Delhi to utilize the expertise and services of Indian Physicians settled in USA in continuing Medical Education and Patient Care in India. The following schemes were planned:-

   1. Continuing Medical Education Scheme (CME Scheme)
   2. Equipment Donation Scheme

1. **Continuing Medical Education Scheme (CME Scheme):** The Medical Council of India has been the nodal agency to co-ordinate these schemes. For CME Scheme, an annual grant in-aid under the Plan Budget is released by the Central Govt., Ministry of Health & Family Welfare. The CME Conferences and type of CME programmes to be held at various places are decided after scrutinizing the applications from institutions

desirous of holding such programmes It may be mentioned that a grant of Rs.50,000/- is given for C.M.E. programmes held with Indian faculty and Rs. One Lakh for faculty including N.R.Is. This grant is used for local hospitality of the N.R.I. faculty and for publication of programme proceedings only. A total of 244 CME Programme were held successfully by various medical institutions/ associations in the country during the year under review

2. **Equipment Donation Scheme:** During the year under review, no offer of donation of medical equipment/books and journals has been received under the Equipment Donation Scheme with the Council. This scheme has become more or less redundant.[107]

Board of Governors: It is the recent development in the organization of the council. The Central Government, by its notification, constitutes the Board of Governors, which consists of not more than seven members; who are supposed to be the person of eminence and unimpeachable integrity in the fields of medicine and medical education and who may be either nominated members or ex-officio members, to be appointed by the central government. The Central Government also appoints the chairperson of the Board of Governors.

Functions of the Board:

The board performs the following functions:

- To exercise such powers and discharge such functions provided by the council under the Act
- To grant independently permission for establishment of new medical colleges or opening a new or higher course of study or training or increase in admission in any course of study, to give the person or college concerned a reasonable opportunity

107. Ibid., pp. 3-7

of being heard as provided under the Section 10A without the prior permission of the Central Government under the Section, including exercise of the power to finally approve or disapprove the same and

- To dispose of the matters pending with the central Government under the Section 10A.[108]

Functions of the Council

The Medical Council of India was established in 1934 under the Indian Medical Council Act, 1933, with the main function of establishing uniform standards of higher qualifications in medicine and recognition of medical qualifications in India and abroad. However the expansion and diversification of medical education in India endowed the council with more function from time to time. It was felt that the provisions of Indian Medical Council Act were not adequate to meet with the challenges posed by the very fast development and the progress of medical education in the country. The later amended that took place (which are mentioned above; in the evolution of MCI) also made the council responsive to other aspects like permitting the new institutions in the field of medical education, regulating maintenance of their standards and of the already existed institution.

The main functions of the Medical Council of India are the following:

1. Establishment and maintenance of uniform standards for undergraduate medical education.
2. Regulation of postgraduate medical education in medical colleges accredited by it. (The National Board of Examinations is another statutory body for postgraduate medical education in India).

108. http://www.mciindia.org/Acts/IMC_amendment_act_2010.pdf, Website of MCI

3. Recognition of medical qualifications granted by medical institutions in India.
4. Recognition of foreign medical qualifications in India.
5. Accreditation of medical colleges.
6. Registration of doctors with recognized medical qualifications.
7. Keeping a directory of all registered doctors (called the Indian Medical Register).

Registration of doctors and their qualifications is usually done by state medical councils.[109]

Assessment of Medical Council of India as a Regulator

Every education system seeks to have a regulatory mechanism which will oversee the functions namely, maintenance of academic standards in that field, will form rules and regulation for the entry of new firms (institutes), will do the monitoring of these institutions and will perform the task of evaluation of their performance, will work to define mode of funding to these institutions, will regulate on their financial matters too, and more importantly will promote the research and development in this specific areas.

The Medical Council of India was established in 1934 under the Indian Medical Council Act, 1933, with the main function of establishing uniform standards of higher qualifications in medicine and recognition of medical qualifications in India and abroad. The Council came into existence as a main body regulating the standards of institutions of medical education and maintenance of the devised standards through the various mediums of regulations of the council. The Council was endowed with more powers and functions over the period of time through the various enactments in order to cater to the present and future needs of medical education. Recommendation

109. http://en.wikipedia.org/wiki/Medical_Council_of_India.

for recognition/de-recognition of medical qualifications of medical institutions and maintenance of Indian Medical Registrar are among the main area of regulation of the Council. The focused areas of Council's regulation in this chapter are as the following:

1. Maintenance of Standards of Medical Education; Inspection at various Levels
2. Maintenance of All Indian Medical Register
3. Regulation of Various Aspects through the Development of Rules and Regulations
4. Code of Ethics
5. Regulation of Teaching Standards

1. **Maintenance of Standards of Medical Education**: The first major function of the Council is to provide approval to the new institutes in the field of medical education. The maintenance of standards of medical education is the main concern while providing approval to these institutes. The Council makes itself sure that the institutes fulfill the required eligibility criteria. The Council carries out the inspection of medical colleges both at Undergraduate level and Post-Graduate level. The council carries out four kind of inspection.

    i. Inspection for starting of medical college

    ii. Inspection for starting Post-Graduate course in an already existing medical college

    iii. Inspection for recognition of MBBS or Post-Graduate qualification

    iv. Inspection for increase of seats in a particular course as per provision of Section 10A for continuance of recognition of qualification

Following are the details of inspections carried out by the Council, given separately at Undergraduate and Postgraduate level.

A) UNDERGRADUATE:

1.	Inspections for Establishment of new medical colleges	= 41
2.	Inspections for renewal of permission	= 96
3.	Compliance Verification Inspections	= 116
	(+Est. +11(2) +Surprise Inspections	
4.	Inspections for Approval of the college	= 13
5.	Inspections for Increase of seats	= 16
6.	Inspections for renewal of permission for increase of seats	= 34
7.	Compliance Verification inspections for Renewal of increase of seats	(+ Increase +11(2) +Surprise)
8.	Inspections for approval of the college for increase of seats	= 02
9.	Pre-PG inspection	= 14
10.	Compliance Verification Inspection for Pre-PG	= 10
11.	As per Court Order inspection held	= 03
12.	Periodical Inspections + Compliance Verification (25+50)	= 61
	Total Inspections	= 423

B) POSTGRADUATE:

i. 423 inspections for approval of starting various postgraduate medical courses at Medical Colleges were carried out subsequent to requests received u/s 10 A of the I.M.C. Act, 1956 through Central Government, Ministry of Health & Family Welfare.

ii. 309 inspections for recognition of postgraduate medical qualification u/s 11(2) of the I.M.C. Act, 1956 were carried out.

iii. 338 inspections for increase of seats in various courses u/s 10A of the I.M.C. Act, 1956 were carried out.

iv. 81 inspections for Compliance verification for recognition.[110]

2. **Maintenance of All India Medical Registrars:** The other major statutory responsibility of the Council is maintenance of All Indian Medical Register. As stipulated u/s 22 of the I.M.C. Act, 1956 the State Medical Councils are required to send information to the MCI regarding registration granted by them. Based on this statistical information the Council maintains and notifies supplement to the Indian Medical Register annually. Total number of doctors registered in the Country up to 31st March 2010 are 7, 97,764. Statistical data from various State Medical Councils including MCI is tabulated.

Registration of Doctors:

Various types of Registration Certificates issued by this Council during the year under review are as under:- [111]

1.	Permanent Registration Certificate	-	2245
2.	Provisional Registration Certificate	-	811
3.	Additional Qualification Certificate	-	1390
4.	Good Standing Certificate	-	1458
5.	Eligibility Certificate	-	2083.

3. **Regulation of Various Aspects through the Development of Rules and Regulations:** The council regulates almost every aspect of medical education in India. It has developed rules and regulation in order to have a constitutional mechanism for the regulation of various aspects; be it regulating teaching eligibility qualification. Be it code of medical ethics, ragging, screening

110. Medical Council of India (2009-10 a.), Annual Report, 2009-10, op. cit., pp.7-8
111. Ibid., pp.8

test regulations etc. the various rules and regulations developed by the Council are:

i. Indian Medical Council Rule, 1957

ii. Medical Council of India Standing Orders

iii. Post Graduate Committee Rules, 1961

iv. Student admitted in access Rules, 1997

v. Graduate Medical Education Regulation, 1997

vi. Teacher Eligibility Qualification, 1998

vii. Establishment of Medical College Regulations, 1999

viii. Medical Council of India Regulation, 2000

ix. Opening of a new or higher course of Study, 2000

x. P.G. Medical Education Regulation, 2002

xi. Screening Test Regulation, 2002

xii. Eligibility Certificate Regulation, 2002

xiii. Code of Medical Ethics Regulations, 2009

xiv. Election of Student Union Regulations, 2009

xv. Prevention of Ragging Regulation, 2009.[112]

4. **Code of Ethics**: The Council has responded to the ethical issues concerning the medical education in India. For this the council has constituted the Ethics Committee. The present day scenario has changed and as a result of the Consumer Protection Act, 1986 made applicable to the practicing physicians, complaints against doctors have increased manifold. The Council received 769 matters of Ethical nature during the year under review. Out of 769 complaints, 254 have been referred to the concerned State Councils/ Authorities for necessary action, 21 of these are awaiting clarification/details from complainants and/

112. www.mciindia.org.in, op. cit.,

or comments from the concerned Doctors etc. while 494 complaints stand disposed by this Council.[113]

5. **Regulating the Teaching Standards:** The Council in order to promote quality teaching in medical education has devised Teaching Eligibility Qualification Sub-Committee. Through this the Council has prescribed minimum qualifications and teaching experience for recruitment of teachers in a medical college and further promotions in the teaching cadre. The matters, which cannot be decided by the appointing authorities (i.e. Universities or colleges etc.), are referred to this Committee for consideration.

Critical Evaluation

The Council has been a promoter of excellence in the field of medical education and responded to the expansion of medical education as well. The Council takes measures from time to time in order to maintain the standards of medical education. It has done this through the medium of inspection carried out for the various purposes. But the Council faced the criticism because of the cases of misconduct that became the headlines of the newspapers.

The main areas on which Medical Council was criticized are:

1. Flaws in the inspection process
2. Involvement in corrupt practices
3. Deterioration of standards of medical education
4. Violation of medical ethics
5. Inefficiency of the Council

1. **Flaws in the Inspection Process:** The very first area of criticism was about the inspection carried out for the purpose of

113. Medical Council of India (2009-10 a.), Annual Report, 2009-10, op. cit., pp. 6

maintenance of standards of medical education. The studies revealed that the inspection became a formality as sub-standard institutes were also provided approval by the Council. The inspections by the Medical Council of India (MCI) in both government and private medical colleges for renewal of their recognition once used to be a big task for those inspecting as well as those being inspected. But with the MCI itself relaxing norms in favor of the private colleges these inspections have gradually becoming a ritual. MCI does not have enough qualified inspectors as of now to conduct strict and long duration inspections. Also the government is opening up the health sector for privatization. But everyone seems to forget the brutal reality that such superficial inspections will only result in substandard medical education and naturally production of substandard doctors which will ultimately result in poor health care putting the already needy patients thronging the medical colleges in getting the required facilities.[114]

2. **Involvement in Corrupt Practices:** Another case criticized the role of Board of Governors as it was observed that the Board was involved in corrupt practices. When the Bill for seeking the extension in the tenure of Board of Governors was passed in the Parliament this year, the process was preceded by the protest from various members of parliament who protested against the alleged role of Board in the corrupt practices. Maintaining that the Board was "making a mockery of all rules," Ms. Maneka Gandhi went on to say the CBI had conducted inspections of 10 institutions and found "gross irregularities" including submission of fake or forged certificates by faculty members, fudging of records on clinical materials, and infrastructure deficiency. Such findings should have led to cancellation of their

114. Times of India(2012e), "Medical Council of India not very strict in holding the recognition inspection", June 14, New Delhi

permits but the colleges were allowed to admit fresh batches of students, she said.[115]

3. **Deterioration of Standards:** The Council was criticized for deteriorating standards of medical education as cases of its members, indulging in the corrupt practices came to light. The MCI was dissolved by the President of India on 15 May 2010 following the arrest of MCI's president Ketan Desai by the CBI on 22 April 2010. Desai and three others were arrested for allegedly accepting a bribe to permit Patiala-based Gyan Sagar Medical College to recruit a fresh batch of students without having adequate infrastructure. Desai, alleged middleman J. P. Singh and doctors Sukhwinder Singh and Kanwaljit Singh have been booked under the Prevention of Corruption Act.[116]

4. **Violation of Medical Ethics**: The recent criticism was brought into light by a popular reality show these days " Satyamev Jayate" in which cases related to medical profession; violation of medical ethics and malpractices adopted by the different hospitals of the country were discussed. The reason behind these cases was the negligence of the regulatory authority or ignorance of the Medical Council to these kind of happenings. Doctors have demanded an apology from Aamir Khan, for having highlighted medical malpractices on a TV show. However, the fact of the matter is that while corruption in public sector and government has always been the focus of media, corruption in private clinics is seldom brought out. Catastrophic illness in the family is the number one reason for rural indebtedness. Healthcare expenses have become prohibitive even for upper-middle-class families. The most important reason for expensive

115. The Hindu (2012a). "Lok Sabha passes MCI Board extension Bill despite Trinamool saying 'no'", May 7, New Delhi
116. http://en.wikipedia.org/wiki/Medical_Council_of_India

and uncertain healthcare has been corrupt health practice in India. Consider a real case of a person who met with an accident near Electronics City, located on the outskirts of Bangalore. The patient was lying in a pool of blood and many IT professionals passed by. No one stopped to pick him up in a car, for fear of loss of time and later mindless police investigations and prolonged court procedures. A rickshaw driver picked up the patient. He could have taken the patient to Nara-yana Hrudayalaya which is just two km from the place of accident. The driver, however, decided to take him through the by-now infamous Bangalore traffic for over 25 km, to a hospital in the city centre. That hospital pays Rs 3,000 to a taxi driver for bringing a serious patient. The misuse did not stop there. The hospital authorities called for the patient's wife. She rushed in the next half hour. The hospital charged Rs 3 lakh to her credit card as advance payment. A credit limit of Rs 3 lakh is rich by Indian standards. But she was not allowed to see her husband, and had to wait anxiously for over 45 minutes. She could not bear it anymore and barged into the hospital room. The technicians were repairing the ventilator. She immediately shifted her husband to another hospital. The doctors tried to revive the patient's brain for 15 days, but did not succeed. The unethical practice of hospitals encouraging incentive payments to taxi drivers goes unabated. The result could be fatal for the patient. This can happen to any one of us in any city. What else do hospitals do?[117]

This was only the one case many cases are reported of malpractices carried out by the medical institutes, doctors, hospital and Council but went unnoticed. This however describes the misery of the regulation.

117. Times of India (2012f), "Shaming the Hippocratic Oath", June 4, New Delhi

5. **Inefficiency of the Council:** In a complete overhaul aimed at cleansing the medical education system in the country, a task force of the Union Health Ministry has decided to scrap all regulatory bodies, including the Medical Council of India, Dental Council of India, Pharmacy Council and the Nursing Council. 'Medical education today is dictated by bank balance and caste. The existing Councils, besides being unwieldy, have failed to provide a synergistic approach. There is an urgent need for innovation in health-related education. It is unfortunate that medical seats are auctioned in front of students today. This is the best surgical solution for cleansing the system," a source told Times of India (TOI). The report which was discussed with Prime Minister Manmohan Singh on August 26, 2009 by the task force states: "Professional councils such as the MCI/ Nursing and Pharmacy Councils have been set up to regulate the practice of their respective professions, including education. However, many of these councils have drawn criticism from all sections of society and got judicial censure on several occasions."[118]

Conclusion

The Medical Council of India has been regulating all the main areas relating to medical education and has the main responsibility of maintenance of standards of medical education. The Council has developed the various rules and regulations in order to be responsive to the various developments taking in the field of medical education. The Council has constituted some important Committees and Sub-Committees to deal with some important aspects like finance, teaching standards and medical ethics. But the Council faced the criticism because of the cases of misconduct that became the headlines of the

118. Times of India (2009), "MCI scrapped, single council for medical education", August 28, New Delhi

newspapers. The Council's inspection process has been the centre of criticism as the cases revealed that the Council has been compromising on this aspect. The violation of medical ethics and unresponsiveness of the Council in this area has further diluted the image of the Council.

5

Summary, Conclusions and Policy Prescriptions

Introduction

Regulation in the field of higher education has been provided by many regulatory bodies for various areas of higher education. However, in our scope of study we have discussed three major regulatory bodies; UGC, AICTE and MCI. How these bodies have fared so far when it comes to assess their performance in relation to their assumed role is what we have analyzed in different chapters on these bodies. These regulatory bodies have been praised or criticized on many accounts. This chapter contains summary, a brief account of regulating higher education, regulating bodies, objectives, research methodology, the major conclusion and suggestions in order to improve the working of these organization.

Summary

Regulating Higher Education

Regulation has been observed as a controlling factor that concentrates on price-setting, better service delivery, and better trading standards and makes regulation for the entry of new firms in the area of socio-economic goods. Now taking the institution of higher education, the need of regulatory mechanism grows further in this arena. Higher education is no longer perceived as an acquisition of a degree but an instrument to obtain sufficient knowledge and skills so as to function as a productive member of the society. The structure and delivery of higher education is changing, including the coming up of new types of educational institutions and an increasing use of technology that allows institutions to operate on a national and global scale. Also, Higher education has explicitly acquired an economic value in today's knowledge economy. All these changes have resulted in growing demand for increased accountability.[119] The commercialization, privatization, liberalization and globalization and service delivery aspect were among the rationale that demanded regulation of higher education system.

Regulating Bodies

The system of regulation in India saw the emergence of different regulatory bodies for various field of higher education in India. The higher education institutions in India are regulated by many statutory agencies such as, University Grants Commission (UGC), the All India Council of Technical Education (AICTE), Bar Council of India (BCI), Council of Architecture (COA), Indian Nursing Council (INC), Medical Council of India (MCI), National Council on Teacher Education (NCTE), Pharmacy Council of India (PCI), Distance Education Council (DEC) and so on. In addition, there are regulations of the institutions by Central and State universities as well as by the Directorates of College and Technical Education in each State, leading to undesirable cubicalization of knowledge, unwarranted fragmentation of disciplines and separation of knowledge from application and skills.[120]

---

119. Pawan Aggarwal (2006), "Higher Education in India; Need for Change", Working Paper no. 180, Indian Council for Research on International Economic Relations, *New Delhi*

120. Government of India (2008 a), *"Report of 'The Committee to Advise on Renovation and Rejuvenation of Higher Education", Department of Higher Education, Ministry of Human Resource Development, New Delhi.*

Objectives of the Study

Following are the objectives of the study: to

1. Study the working of University Grants Commission(UGC), and evaluating the role UGC as a regulator
2. Describe the working of All India Council for Technical Education(AICTE), and evaluating the role AICTE as a regulator
3. Study the working of Medical Council of India(MCI), and evaluating the role MCI as a regulator
4. Recommend policy prescription for improving effectiveness of regulatory bodies.

To analyze the recommendation of various reports in lieu of National Commission for Higher Education in relation to the existing system of regulation.

Research Methodology

The study is based on secondary data. Secondary data has been collected from the sources such as annual reports of UGC, AICTE, MCI, National Knowledge Commission, Yash Pal Committee Report, Five Year Plans, publications, newspapers, research journals, articles, various other reports and doctoral dissertations. Secondary data has also been collected through the vast resources of World Wide Web.

Major Conclusions

In the scope of present study three main bodies; UGC, AICTE and MCI have been covered. The regulatory mechanism in higher education can be viewed as a system in transitional phase because of the wide consensus emerging out for the set up of one National Regulatory Commission for regulating all the areas of higher education, supervising all these bodies. The National Knowledge Commission's reports and that of Yash Pal Committee have one the one hand has criticized the existing system of regulation and have on the other hand provided convincing and strong arguments for setting up of one National Commission for Higher Education and Research. The NKC has termed it as Independent Regulatory Authority for Higher education (IRAHE). Given the national aspirations for greater and equitable access to knowledge it is essential that the regulatory system propel the growth in the right direction. A well-designed regulatory system helps to promote a high degree of professionalism in managing higher education institutions.

A highly over-regulated system consists of interference by multiple agencies which tend to stifle innovation and creativity, increase inefficiency and breed corruption and malpractices. An under-regulated system encourages exploitation, contributions to disorder and erosion of social justice. Therefore, it is important to design a balanced and all encompassing regulatory mechanism that is overarching, transparent and ensures accountability which would evoke confidence in the academic institutions and academic body at large. It needs to be realized at this stage that the creation of bodies like the UGC, AICTE, ICAR, and MCI and so on has certainly helped in focusing attention on general and specialized areas. It has, at the same time, fragmented the higher educational sector in the country from a policy perspective. This has, on many occasions, created situations where different agencies have taken different views on issues of regulation and promotion of higher education. While the need to pay focused attention on some important aspects of education remains valid, it is imperative that a holistic view of education is not lost. In terms of regulation what it requires is a De Novo regulatory body under which the various functions of existing regulatory agencies would be subsumed. The powers vested currently in these multiple agencies for regulating creation of academic institutions and their content would be also taken over by the proposed apex regulatory body.[121]

The UGC was formally established in November 1956 as a statutory body of the Government of India through an Act of Parliament for the coordination, determination and maintenance of standards of university education in India. However the scope of University Grants commission's activities has experienced a broadened change over the time as it was entrusted with more functions and activities. The overall and major function of UGC at the time of its constitution was only pertaining to the allocation of grants-in-aids to the universities from the public funds but later on it was endowed with function by which it supervises almost all administrative and educational facets functions of higher education institutions.

Assessing the role of the UGC, The Yash Pal committee report has praised the Commission as it has stated in the report that only a few organizations such as the UGC took major initiatives in fostering educational innovations such as setting up of Inter-University Centres to facilitate national synergy in research efforts among universities and to optimize the investments in sophisticated research infrastructure. The creation of country-wide educational communication facility through multiple platforms and creating large scale contents; the setting up of national network of libraries including e-journals for convenient access to higher educational institutions across the country; special incentives to advanced centres of research; and additional resources to institutions with potential for excellence were some of the other initiatives of the UGC in the recent past.

However the UGC failed in areas like regulating the quality of higher education. For example relating the past many issues like deemed universities cropped up which provide enough empirical evidence of not a good governance of the UGC. The reports of Yash

---

121. ibid

Pal Committee and National Knowledge Commission have also cited that congestion of work, over work-load and regulating every aspect of the higher education are the reasons why UGC has failed to perform its actual role, efficiently. The political interference in the matters of the UGC and even the rigidity of various governing rules of UGC like regulations related to the financial matters of the university, providing approval to new institutes, interference in the autonomy of higher education institutes has also led to the criticism.

The All India Council for Technical Education (AICTE), set-up in November 1945 as a national level Apex Advisory Body, marches ahead with its mission of developing and promoting quality technical education in the country in a coordinated and integrated manner. The Council is constantly endeavoring to encourage a meaningful association between the technical education system and research and development activities in a concerted effort aimed at nation-building.

The Council deals with all those areas of higher education which comes under the technical education arena. The emergence of AICTE has been viewed as a body which deals with all the areas of technical educations, oversees its expansion and growth, provides sufficient infrastructural arrangement for the expansion of medical education, looks forward to the diversification and advancements in technical educations and is responsible for the promotion of technical education, last but not the least works as a overall regulator in the field of technical education. The Council has been responsive to the above mentioned functions through its various policies and programmes. The Council in order to maintain the standards of technical education in India has been checking out the credentials of institutes of technical education at the time of providing approval to these institutes or through the inspection thereafter. In April 2012, in a bid to crack down on corruption in technical education institutes, the All India Council for Technical Education (AICTE) has cancelled recognition of five engineering colleges affiliated to Rajasthan Technical University (RTU) on grounds of their involvement in malpractices.

The research and development of technical education and its promotion has been given deserved importance in AICTE's programmes over the years. Through Clauses 10 (c) and 10(d) of the AICTE Act, the Council promotes innovations and research and development in established and new technologies; generation, adoption and adaptation of new technologies to meet developmental requirements of the country and for the overall improvement of educational process. Towards these ends, the Council has operated three schemes, namely, Modernization and Removal of Obsolescence (MODROBS), Research Promotion Scheme (RPS) and Nationally Coordinated Projects (NCP).

The Council has been criticized for its involvement in the cases of corruption and these cases showed the Council compromising on the standards of technical education by giving approval to the new institutes. The inspection process was also criticized. It has happened many times that the institutes which were approved by the AICTE lacked on many ground specified in the approval criteria. Another criticism came from the Parliamentary Committee as the Council was termed inefficient because of the employability issues. The Committee has voiced concern over "employability" of students passing out of technical institutions in the country, saying the expected response from the industry is "simply missing". Despite several initiatives taken for meaningful interaction between industry and academia for mutual benefits specific to technical education system, linkages between industry and technical institutions continue to remain weak, the Committee said. It was said that the council was mainly responsible for this failure

The Medical Council of India was established in 1934 under the Indian Medical Council Act, 1933, with the main function of establishing uniform standards of higher qualifications in medicine and recognition of medical qualifications in India and abroad. The Council came into existence as a main body regulating the standards of institutions of medical education and maintenance of the devised standards through the various mediums of regulations of the council. The Council was endowed with more powers and functions over the period of time through the various enactments in order to cater to the present and future needs of medical education. Recommendation for recognition/de-recognition of medical qualifications of medical institutions and maintenance of Indian Medical Registrar are among the main area of regulation of the Council.

The Council has responded to the ethical issues concerning the medical education in India. For this the council has constituted the Ethics Committee. The present day scenario has changed and as a result of the Consumer Protection Act, 1986 made applicable to the practicing physicians, complaints against doctors have increased manifold. The Council received 769 matters of Ethical nature during the year 2009-10. Out of 769 complaints, 254 have been referred to the concerned State Councils/ Authorities for necessary action, 21 of these are awaiting clarification/details from complainants and/or comments from the concerned Doctors etc. while 494 complaints stand disposed by this Council.

The Medical Council was criticized for its involvement in corrupt practices. The MCI was dissolved by the President of India on 15 May 2010 following the arrest of MCI's president Ketan Desai by the CBI on 22 April 2010. Desai and three others were arrested for allegedly accepting a bribe to permit Patiala-based Gyan Sagar Medical College to recruit a fresh batch of students without having adequate infrastructure. The studies revealed that the inspection carried out for the purpose of maintenance of standards of medical education, became formality as sub-standard institutes were also provided approval by the Council. The recent criticism was brought into light by a popular reality show these days " Satyamev Jayate" in which cases related to the violation of medical ethics were discussed and Council's ignorance to these cases was highlighted.

The chapters on the working and assessment of the Bodies; UGC, AICTE and MCI clearly point out the lacunas in the regulation of these bodies.

Policy Prescriptions

The National Knowledge Commission and Yash Pal Committee recommendations have been steering the debate in favour of single independent regulatory commission in the field of higher education. In the light of this dominating disclosure the policy prescriptions in the present study have been divided into two parts. The first part deals with policy prescriptions for improving the existing regulatory bodies in the field of higher education. The second part is devoted to the policy prescriptions covering the proposed National Commission for Higher Education and Research

PART I

Policy Prescriptions Covering Existing Bodies

The regulatory bodies like UGC, AICTE and MCI came into existence providing regulation in different areas of higher education namely general technical and medical education. UGC, AICTE and MCI were praised by many and criticized by many in their performance appraisal. Here we individually discuss the policy prescriptions for improving the functioning of these bodies in relation to their criticism;

1. Policy Prescriptions covering UGC
2. Policy Prescriptions for AICTE
3. Policy Prescriptions for MCI

Policy Prescriptions Covering UGC

The policy prescriptions covering UGC are as under;

1. **Multiplicity of Roles Needs to be More Specific:** The various report criticized the Commission as it has to perform multiplicity of roles and has to regulate each and every aspect of the higher education; research, admission, fee structure, approving universities etc.. However UGC is the only body that was praised by Yash Pal Committee reports but even the reports seeks that the Commission should not be over-burdened with more functions. The National Knowledge Commission Reports also suggested that the role of the UGC will be limited to disbursing public funds.

2. **Barriers to the entry of new institutes:** UGC's regulation in allowing new institutes to enter in the field of higher education is not flexible. The Commission needs restructure its strategy of approval in order to be complementary to the good institutes entering in the field of higher education.

3. **Regulation for Deemed to be Universities:** The provision of 'Deemed to be University' was provided in order to promote those institutes which are faring well when it comes to maintenance of standards and excellence in higher education. The data provided by the Yash Pal Committee Reports says, "Between 1956 and 1990, in 35 years, only 29 institutions were granted the deemed university status. In the last 15 years, 63 institutions were declared deemed universities and particularly in the last 5 years, 36 institutions, excluding RECs, have been notified as deemed universities. However the increase may be because of the expansion of higher education but what has raised the concern of the academic world is the fact that the majority of these institutes are not established with any educational purpose, and they end up only deluding the students. In view

of considerable misuse of the provision for Deemed University status, the granting of such status should be put on hold till unambiguous and rational guidelines are evolved. Institutions wishing to get deemed university status should demonstrate special capabilities as were originally intended and should be rigorously evaluated to see if they fulfill the holistic and universal concept of university outlined in this report.

4. **Restrictive and Destructive Interference in the Finances of Colleges/Universities:** The argumentation carried out by the various reports show the Commission encroaching in the financial autonomy of institutes in mobilization of their financial resources. However this interference needs to be more constructive and positive.
5. **Delayed Decisions:** UGC has been criticized for not efficiently implementing its policies and programmes and not been able to carry its objectives within the stipulated time limit. Grants in most of cases especially Five Years Plans are sanctioned in the third year of plan. It becomes very difficult for the universities and institutes to optimally spend scarce resources within two years of the Five Year Plan. It is suggested that UGC should follow the time frame strictly.
6. **Amending Governing Rules and Regulations:** The Commission needs be more responsive to the developments taking place in the field of higher education and its rules and regulation should be more complementary and flexible in infusing innovation and excellence in the field of higher education.

Policy Prescriptions for AICTE

The policy prescriptions for improving the functioning of AICTE are;

1. **Approval Process should be Objective and Transparent:** The Council has been criticized for unfair practices while approving

the new institutions. The cases of Council indulging in unfair and corrupt practices are on rise. The Council needs to take care of this aspect and should do self-assessment and should work for institutional mechanism favouring objectivity and transparency in the approval process.

2. **Employability Issues:** Technical education has been viewed as a professional education, and the regulator in this field i.e. AICTE which looks to promote the technical education needs to be more pro active in relating technical education with the industry, or developing curricula where there are developed applications of technical education in relation to industry and market so that employability of professional graduates increases from 25 percent to 100 percent.

3. **Maintenance of Standards of Technical Education:** The Council has the main task of maintenance of standards of technical education. The Council which works also through its state level units has been unresponsive or failed to stop and check the mushrooming of ill standards institutes in the field of technical education. It has happened many times that the institutes which were approved by the AICTE later it came to light that the institutes lacked on many grounds. According to a report of the Comptroller and Auditor General of India, each of the 171 new institutions that were audited failed on one or more pre-requisites of the AICTE. The Council should be more responsive in dealing with these kinds of cases. A well structured system of rules and regulation; for the maintenance of standards of technical education, regular inspection in this regard and performa for the entry of new institutes perhaps is the solution.

Policy Prescriptions for MCI

The policy prescriptions for improving the role of Medical Council of India are as under:

a. **Making Approval Process Objective and Transparent:** Inspection is the main medium of the Council through which it maintains the standards of medical education in the higher education. The recent cases of inspection of institutions, seeking approval and where the Council compromised in the inspection on standard of medical education has put the question mark on the sincerity of Council in maintaining the requisite standard. The Council needs to overcome the flaws in the inspection process and should make the inspection process more objective and transparent.

b. **Promoting the Medical Ethics:** The Council has the responsibility of maintenance of medical ethics in the field of medical education and medical profession. The recent criticism brought to the news by the realty show "Satyamev Jayate" showed the ignorance of the Council to this aspect. The Council should be more active in the maintenance of medical ethics and more responsive to deal with the cases of violation of medical ethics.

c. **Structural Reforms:** The report which was discussed with Prime Minister Manmohan Singh on August 26, 2009 by the task force states: "Professional Councils such as the MCI/ Nursing and Pharmacy Councils have been set up to regulate the practice of their respective professions, including education. However, many of these councils have drawn criticism from all sections of society and got judicial censure on several occasions. The Council needs a revamp and needs to introduce structural reforms so that it can efficiently fulfill its mandate.

PART II

Policy Prescriptions Regarding National Commission for Higher Education and Research

The National Knowledge Commission's reports and that of Yash Pal Committee have on the one hand has criticized the existing system of regulation and has on the other hand provided convincing and strong arguments for setting up of one National Commission for Higher Education and Research. The National Knowledge Commission which is of the same view has designated the independent regulatory authority as Independent Regulatory Authority for Higher Education (IRAHE). Given the national aspirations for greater and equitable access to knowledge it is essential that the regulatory system propel the growth and access of higher education in the right direction. A well-designed regulatory system will also help to promote a high degree of professionalism in managing higher education institutions.

In terms of regulation what it requires is a De Novo regulatory body under which the various functions of existing regulatory agencies would be subsumed. The powers vested currently in these multiple agencies for regulating creation of academic institutions and their content would be also taken over by the proposed apex regulatory body namely National Commission for Higher Education (NHCER). The functions of the proposed National Commission for Higher Education according to Yash Pal Committee Report are as under:

It shall be the duty of the Commission to:

1. "Make regulations specifying academic standards and related norms and requirements in regard to the pursuit of knowledge in any field of higher education including professional education and research;

2. Make regulations specifying appropriate norms, processes and structures for accrediting universities and institutions of higher learning and research;
3. Make regulations specifying transparent norms and processes for establishing and winding up institutions of higher learning and research;
4. Make regulations specifying sources, norms and related mechanisms for financing universities and other institutions of higher learning and research;
5. Make regulations specifying norms and related mechanisms for transparent and accountable governance in universities and other institutions of higher learning and research;
6. Monitor all matters relating to the standards of higher education including professional education and research in any field of knowledge through an appropriate national data base ;
7. Report on the state of higher education and research including professional education in all fields of knowledge in the territory of India and its comparison with the state of higher education and research in other countries;
8. Make recommendations that ought to be taken for renovation and rejuvenation of higher education including professional education; and such recommendations may include;
    - i. A vision of higher education to be reflected in a curriculum framework
    - ii. Norms and standards for grading or rating or otherwise benchmarking universities,
    - iii. Measures and norms as well as mechanisms for developing requirements of different disciplines of knowledge,
    - iv. Norms and mechanisms for evaluating costs and price of higher education including professional education,

v. New policies for the growth and strengthening of universities and other institutions of higher learning and research, and

vi. Recommendations in regard to the measures to be taken to prevent malpractices, if any, in any activity relating to universities and other institutions of higher learning and research;

9. Encourage through the creation of an enabling environment for universities to become self-regulatory bodies for the maintenance of standards of higher education and research;
10. Advise the President or Union or State Governments, as the case may be, on policies relating to higher education including professional education and research in any field of knowledge;
11. Develop policies and processes that would create an enabling environment for eligible youth to take up teaching and research as occupation and career;
12. Develop policies and processes that would enable qualitative and meaningful interaction between students and teachers in universities and other institutions of higher learning and research;
13. Develop measures required to lighten the work load of universities in regard to their routine functions so that the quality of time available to universities for research and teaching is meaningfully enhanced, and such measures may include, but not limited to, schemes for gradually enabling colleges affiliated to universities to be independent of such affiliation;
14. Discharge such other functions in relation to the promotion, coordination and maintenance of standards of higher education and research including professional education as the President

may subject to the provisions of any law made by Parliament made in this behalf, by rule specify."[122]

However the report of Yash Pal Committee has also brought out the concern that the proposed transition of regulatory mechanism in higher education is not going to be an easy task. It needs a lot of expertise to give this idea of transition a practical shape. The committee is of the view that the transition can be smoothly handled by availing the expertise already available with the present apex bodies. Transition to the new organizational frame should enhance the people working in the present structures. Maximum care needs to be taken to ensure that the creation of the new apex body does not affect these people adversely. However, this need not be a constraint while deciding the structure of the new body. All this needs very careful analysis of the potential requirements. It is proposed that the job to provide operational frame should be assigned as a project on a consultancy basis to a competent professional organization. A task force would need to be constituted by the Government to work out the details of the process of implementation of the recommendations once they are accepted.

The Government of India has drafted a Bill titled "Higher Education and Research Bill" for setting up Independent Regulatory Commission in the field of higher education. The Bill is pending in the parliament.

122. ibid

Index

Symbols

1933 98, 99, 116
1956 26, 92
1957 103
1986 103
1988 96
(AICTE) 24, 62
(U.G.C.) 26
(UGC) 24

A

academic distinctions 29
academic excellence 65
academic governance 51
academic infrastructure 44
academic institutions 72
Academic Staff Colleges (ACS): 35
academic standards 19, 43-44, 89, 99
accelerating research 87
Access 17
accountability 8, 14, 65
Accountability 17
accreditation 35
Accreditation 17
Accreditation of medical colleges. 99
Accreditation System 42
achieve excellence 45
achieving excellence 46
adequate infrastructure 106
a directory of all registered doctors 99
adopt innovations 44
Adult 50
advancement of knowledge 63
affordability 14
AICTE 14-15, 17-18, 20-21, 23-24, 63-64, 69, 72-74, 77-78, 81-82, 84-86, 110, 112, 115-16, 118, 120
AICTE-INAE 83
AICTE's Vision 65
All India Council for Technical Education (AICTE) 62, 79, 115
All India Council for Technical Education (AICTE): 61
All India Council for Technical Education(AICTE) 112
All India Council for Technical Education regulates 87
All India Council of Technical Education (AICTE) 111

All India Medical Registrars 102
Allocation of funds 42
Allocation of Funds 43
alumni contribution 58
annual budget 77
Approval Process 120
assessment 34-35
Assessment of manpower requirement 73
Assistance for Strengthening 46
assure the quality 11
Autonomous College 44
autonomous colleges 52
autonomous status 44

B

Bar Council of India (BCI) 111
Barriers to the entry 55
Bilateral Exchange programmes 46
breed corruption 113
broadened change 28
broad framework of syllabus 95
budget 96

C

cancellation of their permits 105
capabilities 35
Career Award for Young Teachers (CAYT) 18, 83
cases of corruption 23
cases of exploitation 22
Central Advisory Board of Education (CABE) 62
Centre of Excellence 45
Centres for study of Social Exclusion 50
challenges of expansion 30
check corruption 53
civil society 3
Code of Ethics 100
code of medical ethics 102
collaborations 23
collect information 38
commercialization 9, 24, 111
Commissio 72
communication technologies 14
Composition of AICTE 66
Comptroller and Auditor- General 39
consolidated fund 37
Consortium for Education Communication (CEC) 33
Consumer Protection Act 96, 103, 117
Continuing Education 50
Continuing Medical Education Scheme 96
coordinated development 65
co-ordinate development 65
Coordinate with the States 81
co-ordination 37
coordination 36, 40
corrupt measure 11
corrupt practices 104
Corrupt Practices 105
Council of Architecture (COA) 111
crack down on corruption 21, 79

D

Deemed Universities 52
delivery aspect 9
Dental Council of India 22
details of curriculum 95
deteriorating standards 7
Deterioration of standards 104
Deterioration of Standards 106
determination 36-37, 40
developing policies 3

development 1, 3
developmental requirements 81
Development of Rules and Regulations 102
development of various schemes 19
devised standards 99
disbursed funds 56
disburse funds and grants 37
disburse grants 26
disburse out the funds 75
disbursing grants 28
disbursing public funds 56
Dissemination of knowledge 66
Distance Education Council (DEC) 111
diversification 9, 14, 30, 62, 115
Diversification 17

E

economic development 2-4, 15, 17
economic reforms 9
economy 3
Educational Communication 33
educational innovations 54, 60
education autonomy 8
effective implementation 82
effectiveness in operations 7
effects of globalization 12
efficiency 2
e-governance 51
eligibility criteria 11, 100
Emeritus Fellowship 83
Emeritus Fellowship Scheme 46
Employability issues 86
Employability Issues 86, 121
Encouraging indigenous technology 66
enhancing access 43
enhancing facilities 43
ensures accountability 113
ensuring equity 43
Entrepreneurship Development Cell (EDC) 83
Entry of New Institutes 58
Equal Opportunity Cell (EOC) 48
Equipment Donation Scheme 96-97
erosion of social justice 113
establishment 10
evaluation 41
examination 37
excellence 43
expansion 9, 14, 62
Expansion 17
expansion of the activities 38
expenditure 96
Expert committee 53
exploitation 10
Extension (ACEE) 50

F

Faculty Improvement Programme 41
Failure in maintaining the standards 86
fake degrees/mark sheets 53
Fee mechanism 55
Fee Mechanism 59
Fee Regulations 53
Fee Structure 85
Field outreach (FO) 50
finally approve or disapprove 98
finance 94
Finances of Colleges/Universities 58
financial assistance 41, 43, 46-47
Financial assistance 84
Financial Assistance 83
financial autonomy 120
financial matters 58, 99
financial needs 37

financial position 38
Financing 17
Five Year Plans 25
Focusing on non-formal education 66
foreign engagements 13
Foreign Institutes 85
foreign medical qualifications 99
foreign ownership tag 13
foreign universities 13
Formalism and structural delays 55
Formalism and Structural Delays 57
formulate schemes 75
Framing regulations 28
Functions of AICTE 74
funding procedures 57
funding programmes 48
further promotions 95

G

gender gap 49
generalization 10
General Plan Development Assistance 43
globalization 4, 11-12, 15, 20, 24, 111
Globalization 6, 11
global manpower planning 66
good standing certificates 93
Governing Rules and Regulations 57, 120
governmental intervention 5
Government Departments 72
government intervention 7
granting autonomy 76
grants-in-aid 27, 43, 59
Grants-in-aid 19
Grants-in-Aid 42, 43
grants-in-aids 28, 36
group activities 32

H

higher qualifications 90, 98-99
high quality Institutions 65
holding seminars 50
human capital 2, 4, 15
Human capital theory 2
human research development 32
human resource 21
human resource development 2

I

Identification of Universities 41
imparting relevant education 43
implementation 48
implementation of policies 48
Improvement Programmes 43
improving quality 43
inadequate infrastructure 87
Inclusion of ICT 42
incorrect information 21
increase inefficiency 113
increasing exploitation 7
Inculcating entrepreneurship 66
Inculcating marketing skills 42
Independent Regulatory Authority for Higher education (IRAHE) 113
Independent Regulatory Authority for Higher Education (IRAHE) 123
Indian Education policy 62
Indian Medical Council 93
Indian Medical Council Act 92, 98, 99, 116
Indian Medical Council Rule 103
Indian Nursing Council (INC) 111
Industry Institute Partnership Cell (IIPC) 83

INFONET Digital Library 50
Information and Library Network (INFLIBNET): 33
infrastructural arrangement 78-79
infrastructural facilities 53
infrastructure 21
infrastructure deficiency 105
Innovative Programmes 41
inspection activities 38
Inspection for increase of seats 100
Inspection for recognition of MBBS 100
Inspection for starting 100
Inspection of Institutes 80
inspection of institutions 122
inspection process 109
Inspection Process 104
inspections 22
institutional makeup 12, 20
institutions 6
intellectual luxury 3
interference 10
international competitiveness 3
International Cooperation 41
international student exchange programmes 13
Inter University Accelerator Centre (IUAC) 32
Inter University Center for International Studies (IUC-IS) 34
Inter-University Centers: 32
Inter University centre for Astronomy and Astro-Physics (IUCAA): 32
Introducing ICT 50
investment 3
investment project 2
investments 11

J

Junior Research Fellowship (JRF) 46

K

knowledge economy 6, 14-15, 111
Kothari Commission 8, 64

L

liberalization 1, 5, 9, 111
licensing fees 58

M

maintaining standards 28
maintaining the standards 87
Maintaining the Standards 86
maintenance 37, 40
Maintenance of Academic Standards 79
Maintenance of All Indian Medical Register 100
Maintenance of Indian Medical Register. 93
maintenance of norms 73
maintenance of standards 21, 108
Maintenance of Standards 100, 121
maintenance of uniform standards 98
major policies 18
malpractices 10, 23, 107
Malpractices 79
Malpractices Cell 53
management quota 11
market forces 7
market skills 49
Maulana Abul Kalam Azad Scholarship 47
MCI 25, 110, 112, 118

media communication 33
Medical Council of India 22, 89, 90,-92, 96, 98-99, 108, 116, 121
Medical Council of India (MCI) 105, 111
Medical Council of India(MCI) 24, 112
medical qualifications 98-99
menace of ragging 54
MHRD's supervision 55
migration 94-95
Migration 95
minimum qualifications 95
Ministry of Human Resource Development 64
Minority Communities 47
Mission of AICTE 65
modernization 4, 33
Modernization and Removal of Obsolescence (MODROBS) 18, 81, 116
monitoring 41
Monitoring developments 28
Monitoring the Various Schemes 48
Motivation Workshops 49
Multiplicity of roles 55
mushrooming of fake institutions 42
mushrooming of Fake Institutions 53
Mushrooming of Fake Institutions 52

N

National Assessment and Accreditation Council (NAAC) 34
National Board of Accreditation 72, 76
National Board of Accreditation: 71
National Commission for Higher Education 24
National Commission for Higher Education and Research 118, 123
National Commission for Higher Education and Research (NCHER) 16
National Commission For Higher Education and Research (NCHER) 40
National Commission for Higher Education (NHCER) 123
National Council on Teacher Education (NCTE) 111
National Doctoral Fellowship 83
National Eligibility Test (NET) 42
National Facilities Centre 35
National Knowledge Commission 40, 55, 115, 118-19, 123
National Knowledge Commission report 60
National Knowledge Commission Report 56
National Level Regulatory Authority 17
Nationally Coordinated Projects (NCP) 18, 81
National Policy on Education 69
national policy on education 1986 30
National Policy on Education (1986) 30
National Qualification Authority 57
National Regulatory Commission 112

National Technical Manpower Information System (NTMIS) 84
Nature of governing rules 55
Networking 41
Networking of Institutions 65
network of libraries 33
new innovations 3
new medical colleges 97
new technologies 81, 116
NTMIS 84
Nursing Council 22

O

Objectives of AICTE 66
online application 21, 80
operating mechanisms 64
opportunities 35
organizational designs 7
Organization of AICTE 69
organizing programmes 50
overall funding 43

P

Permanent registration 92
PG Indira Gandhi Scholarship 47
Pharmacy Council 22
Pharmacy Council of India (PCI) 111
physical infrastructure 34
Planned and coordinated development 66
policies 74
Policy decisions 95
policy formulation 51
policy process 84
political democracy 3
poor quality 10
population 2, 4
Postgraduate qualifications 94
power politics 8
prevent commercialization 76
Prevention of Corruption Act 106
price indexation 59
price-setting 6
private sector 1, 3
privatization 5, 10-11, 24, 105, 111
Privatization 6, 9
Process of determination 55
Process of Determination 57
production 2
productivity 3
product standards 6
Professional Councils 122
Professional Courses 63
profit maximization 11
programmes 74
prohibition of donation 38
promote an effective link 75
promote girls education 47
promote innovation 75
promotes innovations 116
Promoting and Supporting Research 46
promoting innovation 87
Promoting innovations 78
Promoting Innovations 81
promoting quality 63
Promoting Social Equity 47
Promoting Women Education 48
promotion 37
promotion of excellence 19
Promotion of excellence 42
Promotion of Excellence 43
Promotion of industry-Institution interaction 66
Promotion of Market Skills 49
Promotion of qualitative improvements 73

Promotion of qualitative research 42
Promotion of Quality 66
proper maintenance 65
proper planning 65, 73
proper utilization of grants 82
providing accreditation 34
Providing affordable education to all. 66
Providing approval 80
Providing Approval 78
providing mechanism 47
public funding 59
public funds 60
public investment 56
public-private partnership 9, 14
public services 8

Q

qualitative improvement 65
quality 2
Quality 17
quality assessment 71
quality assurance 27, 71
Quality assurance 8
quality education 4
Quality Improvement Program 74
Quality Improvement Programme (QIP) 18, 83
quality in research 43
quality management 71
quality teaching 19, 104

R

ragging 102
Rajiv Gandhi National Fellowships 47
Reciprocity with foreign countries 93
recognition of qualification 19
recommendation 37
Registration Certificates 102
Registration of doctors 99
Registration of Doctors 102
regulating bodies 110
Regulating Bodies 111
Regulating the deemed universities 42
Regulating the fee structure 78
Regulating the studies 42
Regulating the Teaching Standards 104
Regulation and maintenance of norms 66
regulation of fees 38
Regulation of postgraduate medical education 98
Regulation of schemes 78
Regulation of Schemes 83
Regulation of Teaching Standards 100
regulation of UGC 42
regulations 38
Regulations 95
regulatory bodies 22-24
regulatory mechanism 6, 8-9, 11, 14, 18, 23, 61, 99
regulatory policies 1
regulatory system 57
Relevance Based Education 50
replies of parliament question 53
research and development (R&D) 4
research facilities 33
research infrastructure 54, 114
research programmes 32
Research Promotion Scheme (RPS) 18, 81
Research Promotion Scheme (RPS) and Nationally Coordinated Projects (NCP) 116

Resource Mobilization 51
Responsibilities of AICTE 73
Reviewing the Performance 54
Rising inequities 7

S

screening test regulations 102
self financing 61
Seminar Grant 83
Sergeant Report of 1944 62
service delivery 8
Service Delivery 7
sex harassment cell 53
skewed growth 7
skill accreditation 82
skill assessment 82
skill development 4, 23, 82
skill development workshops 49
skilled labour force 15
social equity 47
social opportunities 4
social progress 3
societal benefits 15
socio-economic mobility 42, 47
Special Assistance Programme (SAP) 45
Special Assistant Programme (SAP) 43
special grants 43
specified activities 37
Staff Development Programme 83
statement of accounts 39
strengthening of Research 42
structural challenges 41
Structural Reforms 122
sub-standard institutes 19
superficial inspections 105
surprise raids 21, 80

T

Teacher's Eligibility Qualification 95
teaching-cum-research centres 50
Teaching Eligibility Qualification 104
teaching eligibility qualifications 94
teaching experience 95
teaching methods 44
technological advancement 4
Technology forecasting 66
Towards social equity 42
trading standards 6
training programmes 49, 51
Transparent governance 65
Travel Grant 83

U

U.G.C 26
U.G.C. 26
UGC 15, 17, 19, 24, 28, 30, 32-33, 35-36, 40-41, 43-50, 52-56, 58, 60, 64, 110, 112, 114, 118-20
UGC Act 26, 30
UGC-DAE Consortium for Scientific Research: 33
UGC Regional Offices 30
UGC's 34-35, 48, 58
undesirable practices 10
unfair practices 85
uniform standards 92
University Grants 72
University Grants Commission 112
University Grants Commission (UGC) 111
use of technology 7

V

value based education 42, 50
Violation of medical ethics 104
Violation of Medical Ethics 106
Visiting Professorship 83

W

welfare of Minorities 48
Women Education 48
workshops on Human Rights 50

Y

Yash Pal Committee 113-14, 118-19, 123, 126
Yash Pal committee report 54, 60, 114
Yash Pal Committee report 9, 12, 40
Yash Pal Committee Report 13, 25, 112, 123